PENGUIN BOOKS

Letters from Gaza

Mohammed Al-Zaqzooq and Mahmoud Alshaer

Mohammed Al-Zaqzooq is a researcher born in Khan Younis. He studied Arabic language and literature at Al-Aqsa. Mohammed is an active member in literary and cultural organizations shaping Gaza's cultural landscape and the former general coordinator of the 'Utopia for Knowledge' assembly. His poetry collection *The Soothsayers of Khanun* won the Khalili Poetry Award at the First Palestinian Cultural Forum for Creative Writers in 2018.

Mahmoud Alshaer is an editor, curator, and poet who, until October 2023, was deeply involved in cultural work in Gaza, leading initiatives such as Majalla 28 and Gallery 28 and coordinating the cultural programme at Al Ghussein Cultural House in Gaza's old city.

Translators

Ibrahim Fawzy is currently pursuing an MFA at Boston University. He's a graduate of the British Center for Literary Translation Summer School. He was awarded a mentorship with the National Center for Writing, the UK (2022/2023). His translation of Khalid Al-Nasrallah's *The White Line of Night* won a 2023 English PEN Presents award. He's a 2024 ALTA Travel Fellow and was awarded a 2024 Global Africa Translation Fellowship.

Osama Hammad is a literary translator based in Egypt. He holds a Professional Diploma in Media and Audiovisual Translation from the School of Continuing Education at the American University in Cairo. He has published several translated short stories and articles in both Arabic and English, as well as collaborated on translating two books into Arabic. Osama is a contributor to *Arblit, Boring Books,* and *The Antonym* magazine.

Soha El-Sebaie is an Egyptian freelance translator. She has translated more than a dozen books in a variety of genres, including comparative literature, anthropology, history, art, self-help, fiction, and literary nonfiction.

Enas El-Torky graduated from the Department of English Language and Literature at Ain Shams University, where she earned her PhD. She has published several translations and was shortlisted for the ArabLit Story Prize.

Mervat Youssef is an Associate Professor of Arabic. She holds a BS from the University of Helwan in Cairo, an MS from South Dakota State University, and a PhD from the University of Iowa. Her research interests include media constructions of identity, especially in relation to news coverage of Middle Eastern affairs.

Alaa Alqaisi is a Palestinian translator, writer, and researcher from Gaza, who is deeply passionate about literature, language, and the power of storytelling to bridge cultures and bear witness to lived realities.

Hazem Jamjoum is a cultural historian completing his doctorate at NYU, and an audio curator and archivist at the British Library.

Marina Ashraf is a freelance translator.

Wiam El-Tamami is an Egyptian writer, translator, editor, and wanderer. She has spent many years moving between different cultures and communities.

Hadeer Mohamed is a freelance translator based in Cairo.

Nancy Roberts is a multi-award-winning freelance Arabic-to-English translator and editor. In addition to novels, she enjoys translating materials on political, economic and environmental issues, human rights, international development, Islamic thought and movements, and interreligious dialogue. Nancy lived across the Middle East for twenty-five years in Lebanon, Kuwait and Jordan, and is now based in the Chicago suburbs.

Haytham El-Wardany is an Egyptian writer and translator. He lives and works in Berlin and writes short stories and experimental prose.

Mariam Naji is a freelance translator.

Basma Nagy is an Egyptian writer, translator, and cultural coordinator. Her short story collection, *Replica Archive*, won an AFAC grant and was shortlisted for the Sawiris Cultural Awards (2022). She has translated notable literature and sociology works for various Arabic publishers and contributed essays to leading cultural platforms.

Luke Leafgren is an assistant dean of Harvard College, where he also teaches a course on translation. He won the Saif Ghobash Banipal Prize for his translation of Muhsin Al-Ramli's *The President's Gardens*. His most recent translation of *Mister N* by Najwa Barakat, was published in May 2022 by And Other Stories, who also published his translation of *Shalash the Iraqi* in 2023.

Leonie Böttiger (previously Rau) is *ArabLit's* Managing Editor. She is also a doctoral fellow at the MPI for the History of Science (Berlin) and the Berlin Graduate School Muslim Cultures and Societies, working on pre- and early-modern Arabic recipe collections. Her essays and translations have appeared in *ArabLit Quarterly* and online with *Guernica*, *The Recipes Project*, and the *Library of Arabic Literature's* blog.

The ArabLit Collective began as a blog in 2009, founded by M Lynx Qualey. It received the 2017 Literary Translation Initiative Award at the London Book Fair and launched *ArabLit Quarterly* (ALQ) magazine in the fall of 2018. As a crowd-funded collective mostly supported by subscribers, it continues to be a formidable force in bringing Gaza's stories to light and supporting its artists.

Nihal Shafik is a freelance translator.

LETTERS FROM GAZA

BY THE PEOPLE, FROM THE YEAR THAT HAS BEEN

MOHAMMED AL-ZAQZOOQ

MAHMOUD ALSHAER

INTRODUCTION BY ATEF ABU SAIF

PENGUIN BOOKS
An imprint of Penguin Random House

PENGUIN BOOKS

Penguin Books is an imprint of the Penguin Random House group of companies whose addresses can be found at global.penguinrandomhouse.com

Published by Penguin Random House SEA Pte Ltd
40 Penjuru Lane, #03-12, Block 2,
Singapore 609216

First published in Penguin Books by Penguin Random House SEA 2025

Anthology Copyright © ArabLit Quarterly & Books, 2025

All rights reserved

10 9 8 7 6 5 4 3 2 1

The views and opinions expressed in this book are the authors' own and the facts are as reported by them which have been verified to the extent possible, and the publishers are not in any way liable for the same.

Please note that no part of this book may be used or reproduced in any manner for the purpose of training artificial intelligence technologies or systems.

ISBN 9789815323726

Typeset in Adobe Garamond Pro by Digiultrabooks Pvt. Ltd.
Printed at Thomson Press India Ltd, New Delhi

This book is sold subject to the condition that it shall not, by way of trade or otherwise, be lent, resold, hired out, or otherwise circulated without the publisher's prior consent in any form of binding or cover other than that in which it is published and without a similar condition including this condition being imposed on the subsequent purchaser.

www.penguin.sg

To the people of Gaza—

To those who have endured unimaginable loss,

To those who continue to resist with their words, their art, and their lives,

To those who are no longer with us, but whose voices echo in these pages,

Moreover, to the future generations who will carry these stories forward.

This book belongs to you.

Table of Contents

Publisher's Note   *xi*
Introduction   *xv*

No Answer to Satisfy   1
Tell the Sun Not to Blaze So Bright   61
The Sea, Slow and Tired, Carries Me to the Harbour of the Sun   115

Afterword   *181*
Acknowledgements   *185*
Letters to Gaza   *188*

Publisher's Note

All the writings have been completed and shared over the fifteen months following October 2023. Our contributors have endured relentless challenges since submitting their writings, making it difficult to stay connected due to severed communication lines and multiple displacements. As a result, in some cases, author details have been compiled from preexisting information and may not reflect their current location or circumstances. We have unfortunately not been able to establish contact with two of our incredible writers, Sara al-Assar and Basma al-Hor, post receiving their writings, and we continue to pray for their well-being and remain grateful for their contributions.

To provide context to the writings, there are references to certain historical events and global positionings. All references in the book are made in accordance with the UN Resolutions that define the events which have unfolded vis a vis the ongoing conflict.

The Israeli-Palestinian conflict has been addressed through multiple UN Security Council resolutions and international legal rulings:

> UN Security Council Resolution 242 (1967) calls for Israeli armed forces to withdraw from territories occupied during the conflict. Respect for the sovereignty, territorial integrity and political independence of every state in the region.[1]

---

[1] United Nations Security Council. *Resolution 242 (1967), Adopted by the Security Council at Its 1382nd Meeting on 22 November 1967.* 22 Nov. 1967. United Nations Digital Library, https://digitallibrary.un-.org/record/90717. Accessed 18 Feb. 2025.

> UN Security Council Resolution 446 (1979) deems Israeli settlements in the occupied Palestinian territories as illegal and an obstacle to peace.[2]
>
> UN Security Council Resolution 2334 (2016) reaffirms that Israeli settlements in the West Bank and East Jerusalem are violation of international law.[3]
>
> The International Court of Justice (2004) affirms that Israel's presence in Palestinian territories constitutes an occupation under international law.[4]

The Nakba, meaning catastrophe in Arabic, is a term used for the forced displacement of Palestinians from their homes, and dispossession of homeland during the 1948 Arab-Israeli War. Several UN resolutions address the Nakba and its aftermath:

> UN General Assembly Resolution 77/23 called for the commemoration of the 75th anniversary of the Nakba on May 15, 2023, and requested the Division for Palestinian Rights of the Secretariat to organize a high-level event for this occasion. The resolution acknowledged the ongoing impact of the Nakba on Palestinians and emphasized the importance of recognizing this historical event within the United Nations framework.[5]

---

[2] United Nations Security Council. *Resolution 446 (1979), Adopted by the Security Council at Its 2134th Meeting on 22 March 1979.* 22 Mar. 1979. United Nations Digital Library, https://digitallibrary.un.org/record/1696. Accessed 18 Feb. 2025.

[3] United Nations Security Council. *Resolution 2334 (2016), Adopted by the Security Council at Its 7853rd Meeting on 23 December 2016.* 23 Dec. 2016. United Nations Digital Library, https://digitallibrary.un.org/record/853446?v=pdf. Accessed 18 Feb. 2025.

[4] International Court of Justice. *Legal Consequences of the Construction of a Wall in the Occupied Palestinian Territory.* 9 July 2004, https://www.icj-cij.org/public/files/case-related/131/131-20040709-ADV-01-00-EN.pdf. Accessed 15 Feb. 2025.

[5] United Nations General Assembly. *Resolution 77/23, Commemorating the 75th Anniversary of the Nakba.* United Nations, 2022, https://www.un.org/unispal/document/division-for-palestinian-rights-ga-resolution-a-res-77-23/. Accessed 18 Feb. 2025.

> UN General Assembly Resolution 194 (1948) is a significant resolution to the Nakba, which affirms the right of Palestinian refugees to return to their homes and receive compensation if they choose not to return.[6]

There has been massive infrastructural destruction by Israeli attacks during the 2023-24 war in Gaza. Many schools, colleges, places of cultural importance were damaged, about which the UN stated the following:

> UN experts expressed grave concern over the pattern of attacks on schools, universities, teachers, and students in the Gaza Strip, raising serious alarm over the systemic destruction of the Palestinian education system. With more than 80% of schools in Gaza damaged or destroyed, it may be reasonable to ask if there is an intentional effort to comprehensively destroy the Palestinian education system, an action known as 'scholasticide'.[7]

---

[6] United Nations General Assembly. *Resolution 194 (III), 11 December 1948*, 11 Dec. 1948, https://www.securitycouncilreport.org/un-documents/document/ip-ares-194.php. Accessed 18 Feb. 2025.

[7] United Nations Office of the High Commissioner for Human Rights. 'UN Experts Deeply Concerned over "Scholasticide" in Gaza.' *OHCHR*, 18 Apr. 2024, https://www.ohchr.org/en/press-releases/2024/04/un-experts-deeply-concerned-over-scholasticide-gaza. Accessed 18 Feb. 2025;
United Nations News. 'Gaza: UN Experts Decry "Systemic Obliteration" of Education System.' *UN News*, 18 Apr. 2024, https://news.un.org/en/story/2024/04/1148716. Accessed 18 Feb 2025.

Introduction

by Atef Abu Saif
Minister for Culture in the Palestinian Authority

People often say that Gaza exports oranges and short stories. This literary genre has flourished in Gaza, especially after 1967 when Israel occupied the West Bank and Gaza. Writers found that they had to write short, condensed texts full of symbols and metaphors to avoid being prosecuted by the occupying Israel authorities. Israeli authorities closed all printing shops, newspapers, and publishing houses, leaving authors with the choice of holding onto their texts or travelling to Jerusalem to publish them. This created even more reasons to craft short texts and stories.

But Gaza has not just exported stories. After the Nakba, Gaza remained the only place on the historic map of Palestine to bear the name Palestina, after the West Bank was annexed to the Hashemite Kingdom of Jordan. The founding fathers of most Palestinian factions came from or lived in Gaza. Even the first post-Nakba Writers' Union was established in Gaza, before it morphed into the Palestinian General Union of Writers and Journalists. Ghassan Kanafani attended its first-ever meeting. His novel *What Remains for You* reflects his time in Gaza, although Gaza also appeared in Kanafani's earlier stories, including 'A Paper from Gaza'.

In the last three decades, Gaza has maintained its vivid cultural life. Even during times of tension and war, works of art and literature coming from Gaza found a way to communicate with audiences and readers in the region and abroad. Literary salons became a common phenomenon. Some of these salons were held weekly or monthly, devoted to discussing books, aesthetics, and developments in art and literature. This cultural and literary renaissance was part of the general flourishing of Gaza, despite the unjust siege that Israel imposed on it these last seventeen years. Poetry readings, readers' seminars, book discussions, local book fairs, heritage festivals, and concerts were all part of the daily routine of Gazan life. Theatre, cinema, fine art exhibitions, performance, and art installations gave spirit to a place that the siege tried to kill.

Literary groups became remarkably common. The Al-Karawan cultural group was the first to appear in the late 1990s, and it later extended to other regions. Recent years witnessed the emergence of literary groups in various cities, especially in Khan Yunis, Rafah, and Deir Al-Balah.

But Gaza wasn't famous only for exporting short stories; it also exported thousands of teachers to build the education systems in the Gulf, in Algeria, and in Libya. For decades, illiteracy in Gaza has been close to zero. Yet, for the first time in decades, Gaza's cities will face illiteracy once again, due to Israel's destruction of schools and universities. For the second year in a row, students are deprived of their seats in school.

The 2023-24 war targeted everything in Gaza. Systematically and intentionally, most of the archeological sites, museums, libraries, bookstores, galleries, and monuments were destroyed. Around 200 buildings of historical importance, including churches, mosques, archival centers, old hammams, ancient souqs, and centuries-old palaces were damaged. Most cultural centers and institutions, theaters, and music halls did not survive.

Personal libraries and collections of art and antiquities also disappeared under the rubble of the destroyed buildings. Important and influential cultural figures were also lost in the war. Poets like Saleem Nafar, journalists and writers like Bilal Jadallah, and actresses such as Inas Saqa were killed, among scores of others, including many promising young authors, painters, singers, and actors. And yet this didn't stop Gazans from writing.

***

Now, for the first time, we witness a new genre of war writing in Palestinian literature. Although Palestinians have been living in a continuous conflict since 1948, most of the literary writings elaborating on these events were in the form of resistance poetry or fiction. Even the tendency to recapture the horror and pains of deportation and ethnic cleansing that took place during the Nakba were done in a flashback mode and did not reflect, except in a few cases, a present personal experience. That is, the Nakba literature was not written at the time of Nakba.

Until now, we have not seen the emergence of an of-the-moment war literature. This is the first time that writers, poets, novelists, have written war letters, journals, and testimonies for the purpose of documenting what is happening around them and how their lives have been affected and shaped by it.

For Palestinians, writing is resistance and culture has always been used as a tool of resistance. Through poetry, fiction, singing, painting, the dabke, and traditional embroidery and clothing, such as the keffiyeh, Palestinians have fought back against the efforts to eliminate them. In the late 1970s and 1980s, we would tease soldiers by dancing dabke in the narrow alleys of the camp. The soldiers would grow angry and chase us. Culture was our response.

Yet this is not a book about war. It is a book about human souls that strive to avoid being hunted down by war. It is about how innocents are forced to learn how to survive when everything around them is about killing, destruction, and death. It is through these texts that writers rehumanize a life that war has turned into numbers, figures, and breaking news. There is no news here.

All we have is life regained through writings. We read stories, poems, personal narratives, monologues, dialogues, dreams, and nightmares. We meet the people of Gaza as they are, and as they live their actual lives, not turned into numbers or few words for a news broadcast. We meet Gaza, the city that its inhabitants see as the most beautiful place on Earth.

What we read here is more accurate, human, and honest—and also more horrific and astonishing than what we see in the media. We see human bodies fighting amid corpses, children trying their best to reclaim their childhood, old ladies hardly managing to cross the threshold of survival, mourning, and laughter. These texts do not aspire to anything but to be letters of life, to show the reader how a human can be stronger than any killing machine if he insists on his humanity, and how we can be better when we think of life in the moment that death is trying to catch us.

These letters are life lessons written mostly by those who survived. In a few cases, we read short texts by some authors who did not make it and were killed during the war. We read their thoughts before they were killed. We meet them as they meditate on life and death.

Here, we meet the fresh mornings in Gaza, the walk to the university, cups of coffee with friends in the cafeteria, nights on the beach, gardens, the streets, building, squares, public places, social life, cultural events, personal worries, memories of places, even the boring details of everyday life. They are all present in what seems like an attempt to recapture a place that has gone: that is, Gaza. Contributors lament their place and their memory. And, in rediscovering the past, they reflect on the cloudy future that awaits them. And as they do, they manage to reinstate Gaza and bring it back in their fights against the war, which shoved Gaza toward a labyrinth of oblivion.

Atef Abu Saif is a Palestinian writer, born in Jabalia refugee camp in the Gaza Strip. He has been serving as the Minister for Culture in the Palestine Authority since 2019. He is the author of five novels: *Shadows in the Memory* (1997), *The Tale of the Harvest Night* (1999), *Snowball* (2000), *The Salty Grape of Paradise* (2003, 2006), and *A Suspended Life* (2014), which was shortlisted for the 2015 International Prize for Arab Fiction (IPAF). He is a regular contributor to Palestinian and Arabic newspapers and journals. In 2015, Atef was shortlisted for the International Prize for Arab Fiction, also known as the 'Arabic Man Booker'. In 2019, he relocated to the West Bank and became Minister of Culture for the PA. His books have been translated into various languages, and his writings have also been featured in *The New York Times*, *The Guardian*, *Guernica*, and *Slate*.

NO ANSWER TO SATISFY

Calendar for Another World
by Othman Hussein
Translated by the ArabLit Collective

As these words are written, Day 24 bids itself farewell, casting its crimes in the face of history. In the last two hours of the day, I became aware of a calm that had begun at noon, and which would last until the evening of Day 25. Tomorrow is a new day with a new number, and we do not know what its memory has in store for us.

The sound of drones pervades all things, and over time, it has become a constant buzz that forms the background of our lives and inhabits every aspect of our days.

Bahiya did not ask me to explain any explosions tonight, which might have spoiled her mood, especially since she is humming along to a song she likes and sitting with her phone nearby. Her presence dominates the place.

News comes in a never-ending stream, and the sound of airplanes has not let up since morning. There is much talk about a humanitarian corridor to deliver aid. Is this deceptive calm the one paving the way for the humanitarian corridor?

On the first day of the war, the upward count began. The days take numbers, and it is by their number that they are known. So, for example, my house was hit by artillery shells on Day 3. All the other days are tied to the horror of slaughters that were committed within the span of this day or that. On Day 20, the world witnessed how entire families were erased from the civil registry, following the pattern of the rest of the days that had battered the civil registries, days whose events the world also witnessed, when whole neighbourhoods were wiped from geography and history alike.

October 30, 2023

Othman Hussein, a Palestinian poet based in Rafah, Gaza, has a rich literary background. He co-founded the literary magazine *Ashitar* and established the Ashitar Association for Culture and Arts. He held positions such as the secretary of the Palestinian Writers Union and served as the executive director of the Bisan Media Foundation. He contributed significantly to cultural endeavours. Presently, he directs the Cultural Department at the Palestinian Planning Center. He has published several poetry collections, including *Rafah Alphabet of Distance and Memory* (1992), *The Seas Apologize for Drowning* (1993), *Who Will Cut the Head of the Sea* (1996), *For You* (2000), *The Things Left to the Blue* (2004), *As if I Am Rolling Galaxies* (2012), and *The Victim's Guardian* (2023). His family home was destroyed by the Israeli airstrikes in Southern Gaza. He continued to live in Gaza during the war.

A Siege of Questions and No Answers
by Doha Kahlout
Translated by Haytham el-Wardany

Our night is long. During it we soothe our salty memories, and traverse miles of longing that never dulls. In the daytime we run after a whole set of problems that begin with water and end with a piece of bread dipped in exhaustion. We have no time to wonder: Who am I? How did I end up here? What more do I have to lose to get through these days? Lamenting over a past that they have pledged to steal from us.

We spend whatever remaining time we have going through memories, out of fear that they might be destroyed. We try to follow a never-ending stream of questions and fall asleep with our heads still spinning to find the answers.

How Did All These Questions Pile Up?

On October 7, 2023, the siege of questions around the Gazan people began. Wherever they looked, they saw a stubborn question mark hanging. The Gazans did not understand anything from the events of that day and remained stuck at half past six in the morning with these questions: 'What is going on? What are the consequences?'

The next morning, the occupation forces provided answers to our ears. Clamour of weapons we had never heard of before. Policies of demolishing houses robbed our brains. Inhuman statements put us in heavy dread. When we were still graced with enough electricity to receive the disgraced red tape of breaking news, we sat in front of the TV, reading the news out loud, and asking the familiar question: 'Who do we know there?'

And 'there' is the name of the place the news just announced has been targeted without warning.

Names rushed to our tongues as we prayed that no harm had come to them. Amid the barrage of the news and the struggle to meet the basic needs for survival, a nearby missile shattered the quietness of the moment. You feel numb, as if trapped in a dream, expecting it to dissipate when you open your eyes. But you return to consciousness, hearing trembling voices: 'Are you there? Are your sister and brother with you?'

You have no words, no voice. An unimaginable, mighty fear has swallowed you.

The same scenario repeats with all its details. Seven days of the same questions, fears, and unvoiced calls. You think you have survived the spell of questions and that you have acquired the keys to the answers, no matter how difficult, but a brutal enemy still retains scenarios you don't know of.

On the morning of October 13, the Gazan people woke up to a displacement wrapped in a promise of safety. An official statement from the occupation army asked the inhabitants of northern Gaza to evacuate to the south of Gaza's valley, claiming it was a safe area and that the north was a severe fighting zone. A single question echoed through every house across the Strip: 'Where to go?'

Those with relatives in the south moved without hesitation. Those without anyone packed what they could remember, took important papers, and went with the wind. In the streets, amidst the jam of cars carrying fragments of homes, it was easy to read people's faces, to see their fear, and to sense the heavy burden of questions on their shoulders.

By the roadside, you could see people evacuating to the south on foot. They carried no physical memories from their homes except for some light summer clothes and a mental image of their house, over which they cried every night.

Children asked, 'Where to?' and parents held them, speechless.

Unsafe Stories

In the so-called safe south, unsafe stories unfold. Many mothers carried their children and fled without their husbands or one of their kids. They set up tents of misery, cleaned them, arranged their belongings as best as they could to resemble home, and stood at the entrances, hoping to hear the familiar voice of their missing loved ones.

Ikhlas, 42 years old, lives with her husband and four children in a shelter camp. When you look into her eyes as she cooks, washes clothes, prays, or cares for her children, you can see her eyes asking just one thing: 'How is Mohammed now?' Her son remained in northern Gaza.

This question haunts her heart and mind, and the answer, trembling, comes through a sporadic telephone connection when she is lucky enough to have a network. Ikhlas is just one of thousands with hollowed eyes and suspended hearts.

Fayza, 60 years old, stayed in the north, defying the orders of the occupation forces. She gathered her family and moved from one house to the next, entrusting them to God every moment, and feeling happy when they were around her with their father. The occupation forces woke her up to a nightmare worse than war. Her only son was detained and disappeared. She knew nothing about him for more than 40 days. Her husband was killed. When her son was finally released, the occupation forces relocated him to the south of the Strip, far from her, with no means of communication. Now, she spends her nights alone, accompanied only by perennial distress and untamed thoughts.

You wonder: 'Is one person's pain greater than another's?'

You look at Shorouk's perpetually distant face. At 25 years old, her features remain childlike, but her mouth has forgotten how to smile and her eyes are perpetually filled with tears. She sits silently at her tent's entrance day and night, waving her arms while holding her baby.

Many scenarios come to mind, but the worst is what her mother reveals: Shorouk lost her husband after just one year and three months of marriage. He was kind and quiet, and their home was once filled with kindness and their baby's cries.

In a single moment, the occupation forces turned her past into a memory to mourn. Her mother tells you that Shorouk lost her mind. She waits every day for her husband to return and hold their baby in his arms. Every morning she goes out, and every evening she comes back only to sleep, convinced she will see him again.

Is this certainty or madness?

No Answer Is Satisfying

During our long night, all the postponed questions invade us. They fall from the height of denial to the slippery ground of confrontation; a confrontation we try to avoid all day, but it knows how to claw its way into our memories.

Every photo you scroll through on your mobile or in your mind brings forth a question, once poetic but now crushing: 'Will home be lively again, and will our past days return?'[1] You don't know the answer, but hope deceives you into believing they might.

---

[1] A reference to a verse by the 14th century poet Abdelrahim Al-Boraiy Al-Yamany

The devil of the mind pushes you to question the duration of this war and whether it will ever end. Will this be your life forever? You pray against these thoughts and crack jokes with those around you about your return. Everyone laughs until someone ends the conversation with 'if ever we return.' At that moment, you become consumed by your need for survival and for escaping a war you didn't choose.

You love the land, your home, your work, and your adventures in the streets and alleys of Gaza. The experience of deprivation is too hard to bear again. 'When? With whom? To where?' These are all questions you need to answer if you want to find an escape. You must fully understand that leaving means abandoning all the friendships, memories, and experiences Gaza gave you.

The options are narrow and difficult, leading to loss in both cases and a new beginning. It's a state the world doesn't understand. And when you say 'world,' a heavy question pops up in your mind, a question that no one cares about nor knows the answer to: does the world actually see us? No answer seems meaningful. If it does, then where is it? And if not, what is it doing?

As you reflect silently, you realize that four seasons have passed, and you are in a place that doesn't know you and you don't know it. Autumn ends, then winter, then spring, and we try to get familiar with what was never meant for us, and never will be. Each time, we question our ability to hold on until the next month, but then the next month comes and war tightens its grip even more. We live the same day with the same set of feelings and questions: 'How did the people of Gaza endure all this pain?'

The people of Gaza have lived through days of fear, hunger, and loss. The pain of separation passed like heavy clouds across the sky, but the sun of the next day washed it away. This resilience is not due to a lack of heart, but because the constant stream of painful events hardens you, forcing you to suppress your feelings and breaking your pride, leaving you to weep.

Survival is a daily struggle. It begins with the morning heat glowing in the tent and ends with the biting cold at night.

The whole world knows little of this struggle, except for a few stolen photos and scenes of suffering. The world thinks we've gotten used to it, that we've learnt to cope with the deprivation of life's necessities by finding primitive alternatives. This perception allows the world to rid itself of guilt about Gaza, convincing itself with fantasies of heroism and the myth of enduring hardships. Sometimes, short-lived rescue efforts reach us, and other times, the world listens to our death stories with either astonishment or objection.

While the world sleeps, the people of Gaza face a treacherous occupier and grapple with the mighty question: 'How alone are we?'

Doha Kahlout is a poet and teacher from Gaza. Her first collection of poems, *Ashbah* (Similarities), was published in 2018. She was selected for a residency at Reid Hall in Paris as part of the Displaced Artists Initiative, co-sponsored by the Columbia Global Center and the Institute for Ideas and Imagination, but has not been able to take up her place since the Israeli invasion of Rafah and the closure of its border crossing in May 2024. She is currently in Deir al-Balah in central Gaza Strip, from where she has been sharing her writings.

Windows of Our City

by Beesan Nateel
Translated by the ArabLit Collective

Who am I to think of surviving?

I'm not a bird, I've never held a cloud in my hand, and I don't know how Santa Claus's reindeer fly with a sleigh full of children's gifts.

Who am I to be welcomed into a normal life, with its ordinary sadness over a friend going away or grandparents dying? Where I plant basil on my windowsill, take care of my front doorstep, and splash cups of tea without caring about water shortages? Where I cover my hands with engraved silver rings from Jerusalem, my greatest fear that I'll mislay one of them among the drawers?

I don't think about food supplies as I know very well I'm not hungry, even though I haven't had breakfast. I don't care about the price of cheese, because it's there in the market, and I don't crave a piece of chocolate.

Who am I to escape this death?

I'm not rich enough to pay the $5,000 it costs to arrange a border crossing. My grandfather didn't know that his royal line would inherit a refugee's life, so he spent his sadness between windows of hope that they would return to their land. Apart from a refugee's life, he bequeathed me nothing but hope.

Not even the window. All the windows of our city were shattered, grandfather. The windows were assassinated. And what memory will I carry after survival? To whom will I tell everything that's happening now?

I'll say we survived!

What survival is this?

December 25, 2023

Beesan Nateel is a young writer from Gaza and the author of the children's book *Crazy Luna* (Luna al-Majnoona). Beesan has the most vibrant red hair, and life for her was very different before war. She has since then been displaced from her home and is currently in Deir al-Balah in central Gaza Strip.

Hubb and Harb

by Ahmed Mortaja

Translated by Enas El-Torky

Tonight, I will fall asleep telling myself that the noise outside is fireworks, a celebration and nothing more.

That the frightened screams of children are the gleeful terror of suspense before something long-awaited, like Eid.

Tonight, I will fall asleep scrolling through the photos on my phone, telling myself that my evening out with friends wasn't that great—really, I was bored—so now I'm skimming through memories to pass the time.

I will fall asleep cold and curl into myself and think, don't worry… this is just the price we pay for being hot-(or cold-)natured; I don't know which of those I am, but I tell myself that I have enough blankets and must be getting soft.

Tonight, I fell asleep thinking about love, *hubb*, ignoring the Arabic 'ra', that one flick of the pen that splits love down the middle, turning it into *harb*, war. I told myself that this world, as Milan Kundera once said, can't be taken seriously, even in war. But in love, it's possible.

Tonight, I didn't make any of the usual plans or set goals for the new year. When I flip through the pages of war, this falls under the heading 'Lethargy' on page 87. And 'Powerlessness'.

Instead, tonight I fell asleep doing what I do every night: searching for the chapter on surviving this war, with my self and my sanity intact.

December 31, 2023, 11.45 p.m.

Ahmed Mortaja is a writer born in 1996 in Gaza City. He studied psychology and was actively involved in various cultural organizations in the city. With over seven years of experience as a psychologist for NGOs across the Gaza Strip, he dedicated his work to supporting others. Before the war, he could often be found enjoying pies on the beach with friends—but everything changed after October 2023. On October 28, he survived a bombardment that destroyed his home. Emerging from the rubble, he continued to write.

I Write Lest I Succumb to Savagery

by Mohammed Al-Zaqzooq

Translated by Luke Leafgren

After a great deal of inner struggle and back and forth between me and myself, between acceptance and rejection, belief and denial, and questioning whether it would be worth the effort, I've now decided, 106 days after our sudden and jolting entry into the vortex of war, to begin writing.

For long days I remained paralysed, confused, and doubtful of the reality of what was happening. Even now, I continue to run the gauntlet of the war's endless daily details, which include waiting in long, indescribably humiliating and seemingly endless lines for a few loaves of bread, a gallon of drinking water, or a gas cylinder to spare us having to sit in front of a wood stove to cook our daily meals. And then there's the ordeal of following the constantly accelerating events that rip madly throughout the various parts of Gaza. I continue to run in vicious circles whose convoluted details and cruel scenes have occupied my days in their entirety. Meanwhile, I'm given no real opportunity to reflect on the events, which after growing ever greater, have turned all forms of life in Gaza into an endless hell.

Exhausted after a long, sorrowful day, I fell quickly into a deep sleep, until around six-thirty the following morning all hell broke loose. The sounds of missiles suddenly came rushing in from everywhere—huge missiles in large numbers making terrifying sounds that woke my wife and our three little boys, Baraa, Jawad, and Basil, who were sleeping in their room. I found myself rushing towards them, trying to calm them and soothe the fear that had overtaken them and their mother. Terror was written all over their faces. The sounds of missiles and explosions went on nonstop for more than half an hour, during which one question kept running through my head. It was a natural question, but one that no one could answer at the time: What is happening!?

The sounds gradually subsided, replaced by the voices of the people who filled Hamad City, where I live, in the Khan Yunis Governorate. It was such a cacophony, I couldn't understand what anyone was saying. I rushed down the stairs of my apartment building to figure out what had happened. There had been an unexpected, widespread attack on all the settlements and military installations adjacent to the Gaza Strip, something that had never happened before throughout the entire Palestinian–Israeli conflict. I saw people in the streets rushing every which way. Some were driving off, others were hurriedly buying groceries, and others were looking for transportation to take them to where their relatives lived. In the successive wars the people of Gaza have experienced, it's been the custom to gather in a single-family home in an attempt to feel more secure. As the neighbourhood was swept by a massive wave of chaos and tension, I stood there, dazed amidst the confusion, motionless and silent.

Finally, I went back up to the apartment and told my family that a war had begun, and that we would have to decide whether to evacuate the apartment as others were doing and move to the family home in the Khan Yunis camp, or stay where we were. There was a discussion between me and my wife Ola, who refused to leave. At the time, I couldn't make any decisions or think clearly, as the general atmosphere was one of fear, confusion, and conflicting reports; the entire event had come as a shock. As I sat there immersed in my stupefaction and fear—which had gradually begun to intensify—with every passing minute, we were realizing more clearly the truth of what had happened.

My mobile phone rang; it was my older brother, who also lived in Hamad City, sounding fearful and uneasy. He had more accurate news than I did, as numerous reports had been circulating, with people not knowing what to believe. Clearly very tense, he told me that what had happened would mean a long, brutal war, and that we mustn't stay where we were. Rather, we would have to get moving right away and go to the family home in the Khan Yunis camp. He had already made up his mind and had moved there quickly with his family. It wasn't actually a matter of urgency for people to leave Hamad City during the initial hours following the event. However, because the city had recently been established in a location that was relatively isolated from the heart of Khan Yunis, people felt obliged to evacuate quickly and head for the city center, where there were hospitals, markets, and UNRWA schools that had served in wartime as shelters for the displaced.

After a brief, hushed discussion with my wife, we decided to vacate the apartment and go to the family home in the Khan Yunis camp. This was my first displacement.

After hurriedly packing a suitcase with clothes, some blankets, and another small bag with our IDs and passports, we were ready to leave. It wasn't easy to find a taxi to take us to the Khan Yunis camp, as many people were doing the same, and taxis in Hamad City weren't available in sufficient numbers to transport large numbers of families. So, I called the city's taxi office, trying to get a private car to transport us with our bags. The office told me it would take the car thirty minutes to get to us. It would normally have taken only three to four minutes, but due to the intense rush of families wanting to leave, we had to wait the full half hour, which felt like an eternity.

I don't know why I was in such a hurry, when we still hadn't had a chance to take in what had happened. Maybe I felt the need for an honest talk with my father and my brothers, so that we could work together, first in taking in the reality of what had happened, and then in trying to anticipate outcomes and share our fear, which had begun escalating to the point where it was unmanageable.

When the taxi finally arrived, I quickly loaded the bags into the trunk and helped the children to get in, and we were off. The scenes along the way were unbelievable: Israeli army jeeps on the roads surrounded by people with everyone in a daze, military vehicles speeding madly in all directions, and columns of smoke rising along the length of Salah al-Din Street to the east. People's conversations sounded like something you'd hear in a film script. There were four soldiers lying on the ground, and we were told that a number of people had entered Israel military facilities and settlements. The reports were beyond belief, and with every new report, there was a growing sense of dread, trepidation, and bewilderment. When the car reached the Khan Yunis camp, where our family lived, the neighbourhood was in a state of high alert, and relatives and neighbours were gathered in the street. Military jeeps were roaming all the streets, and the sound of gunfire was everywhere.

I had the urge to rush into the house without getting into conversations with the relatives and neighbours who had gathered in groups and pairs, here and there. Inside, I found my father and all my brothers, my mother, and my sisters, and everyone in a frightened daze. We didn't want another war. Why had this happened? Israel was going to burn Gaza to the ground. The atmosphere was charged with tense anticipation. Without saying anything, I sat down and lit a cigarette, filled with disbelief and dread.

The family meeting alleviated the fear that had come over us during the hours immediately following the event. But in truth, our fear was justified. We understood the magnitude of this event better than anyone else, and we were more capable than anyone else of imagining what form the coming war would take. Still, it far exceeded what we could ever have anticipated. As we watched television during the first day of the unfolding events, the scenes we saw were surreal. News reports were pouring in at an accelerating pace, while hearsay, reactions, analyses, claims, and counterclaims spread like wildfire. We all expected to hear the roar of warplanes and the sound of explosions, and we didn't have long to wait. The war began with violent, intense Israeli raids, while Khan Yunis, like other areas throughout the Gaza Strip, witnessed a night in which Israeli bombardment continued nonstop for long periods.

In the space of a single hour, we heard more than five explosions, some louder and some softer, depending on how near or far they were from us. Every raid would leave huge numbers of martyrs in its wake, turning entire families into items of breaking news that were soon followed by scores of others. In the beginning, the impact of hearing of the deaths of entire families was excruciating. But as we grew accustomed to hearing such reports day in and day out, we began treating them as one of the countless quotidian details steeped in misery, suffering, and pain that would shape our reality for long successive days that have seemed to stretch into eternity…

Mohammed Al-Zaqzooq is a researcher born in Khan Younis in 1990. He studied Arabic language and literature at Al-Aqsa University and is a contributor to various Palestinian and Arab platforms. Mohammed is an active member in literary and cultural organizations shaping Gaza's cultural landscape and the former general coordinator of the 'Utopia for Knowledge' assembly. Currently, he coordinates community library and youth teams at the Tamer Foundation for Community Education. His poetry collection *The Soothsayers of Khanun* won the Khalili Poetry Award at the First Palestinian Cultural Forum for Creative Writers in 2018. Mohammed has ardently worked alongside Mahmoud Alshaer to bring all the poets and writers together to aid this collection. Despite the challenges with communication, he has consolidated the most authentic and heart wrenching writings which can bring us somewhat closer to understanding the emotional and physical toll of this horrific time.

How Did You Spend Your Day?

by Beesan Nateel

Translated by the ArabLit Collective

Early in the morning, I shook off a fear that had wrapped itself around me at night, as the sounds of bombing continued to reverberate deep inside my body.

I sat and contemplated everyday domestic sounds, searching for something within them that might contain a ceasefire. I imagined carrying suitcases towards my house, and only my house. On my way there, I wondered what condition it might be in. I prayed that the chickens would still be there, alive, chasing the neighbour's goose. I prayed that my father would be there, leaving out some of the leftovers of our Friday lunch for the neighbourhood dogs, and all the while our cat would be there too, perched with her kittens on the bulging roots of the olive tree, stalking the birds flying around them.

It would be a day on which I hugged the stoic tree in front of our house.

How did you spend your day?

Sleeping.

I worry that I will get used to displacement. I fear that the very idea of calm is safety is now being fixed as far away from our house. I flee my feelings by sleeping, hurtling towards my true subconscious; I relive my reality while asleep.

How did you spend your day?

Being scared.

I am searching for the meaning of our lives—of life—in war.

Nothing has any meaning except imagining what will happen to us and our bodies when the bombs fall.

> How will we die? In one piece, two pieces…three? Will we be just body parts?
>
> Where will our blood splatter?
>
> How does death look like at that moment?
>
> Will there really be angels checking how faithful we were when alive?
>
> Who cares if we die?
>
> How will others know what happened to us?
>
> How long will it take for them to hear that we've died?
>
> What picture and text will be used to sum up our lives?
>
> What will our lives look like in just a picture and some text?
>
> *And*
>
> What about our dreams, our hearts, our memories?
>
> Our past and your present?

How did you spend your day?

Searching for answers.

I wish I could finish writing the whole story…

February 15, 2024

Beesan Nateel is a young writer from Gaza and the author of the children's book *Crazy Luna* (Luna al-Majnoona). Beesan has the most vibrant red hair, and life for her was very different before war. She has since then been displaced from her home and is currently in Deir al-Balah in central Gaza Strip.

The 100 Days

by Mayar Nateel

Translated by Osama Hammad

It has been more than one hundred days of slowly choking, of the war grinding our bones, the world eating the crumbs of our souls. They gather around the table to offer us false hope over the radio.

My name is Mayar. I was supposed to graduate this year and have a simple celebration with my family at home. My cousin used to say to me, 'The moment you graduate, we should have a party.' I used to spend half of my day with my mother in the kitchen, telling her how delicious her cooking was, and the other half wandering in the streets of Gaza. Now, I'm eating canned beans while displaced at someone else's home. I am lucky that my exhausted body has escaped the missiles so far.

I lost my college degree, after the Occupation destroyed my university. I lost our house in the same way, and in a gruesome way I was deprived of my cousin's happiness at my graduation. I am so far from the streets of Gaza that I learnt by heart—so far from being able to reach Sina'a Road, Rimal Road, or Nasr Road. All the roads have become sand and rubble.

The sea was the vessel that carried away all my worries. The seagulls used to take away my anger and travel far away with it. The crows used to eat the ache in my heart. Today, I cannot shake the dust of the days from my body. The heaviness of the war is killing me. The desperate faces of the people eat away my face. I am tired. I try to cry, but my eyelids are a desert for the tents of displaced refugees.

I am heavy with the sadness of my father over our destroyed house, heavy with the hunger of my friends in the north, heavy with the apparition of death that visits us each day. I am so heavy that I cannot even bear eating. I cannot bear sleeping because I am used to sleeping to the buzz of the deadly little *zananas*[2].

I cannot bear looking in the mirror. I am afraid I might see my sadness, afraid that my self would kill me.

February 22, 2024

Mayar Nateel is a writer from Gaza and a talented 23-year-old artist. She recently graduated with a degree in English literature from the Faculty of Arts and Humanities at Al-Aqsa University in Gaza. Mayar has a large, artistic family. Their home, once filled with their father's artwork, has been destroyed, as has her brother's home. They have 'narrowly escaped death several times'. Despite these ongoing challenges, her sister has not given up on her dreams and still hopes to write her first novel.

---

[2] Zanana is an Arabic slang term used by Palestinians in the Gaza Strip. The word means 'buzzing sound' and it is used to refer to the noise produced by Israeli drones.

When We Left Home
by Yousri Alghoul
Translated by Ibrahim Fawzy

My father, his voice thick with sorrow, said: 'Leave Anas and Raouf with me and take Osama and Majd. If death claims any of them, the others will keep your name alive.'

Tears streamed down his face. And so did mine as I hugged him. Anxious. 'Don't worry, Papa. We will be okay,' I whispered.

I went back to my wife, my heart bleeding. Would we die? Would I lose my family and any of my friends? What could I do to shield them from looming death? Was there a way to stop this brutal genocide that was going on in Gaza while the world watched? Big questions that never stopped, questions as immense as missiles targeting one-storey houses, apartment blocks, towers, parks, and even cemeteries. But no answer could offer solace to a soul tormented.

By then, I had been displaced five times. I had left my old house to live in my new one; even if only for once. I built it brick by brick and spent every penny I had on it. I argued with the lazy workers; I made friends with neighbours from all walks of life. It was two floors, and when each floor was completed, I celebrated, giving out sweets and shawarmas to the workers and my friends.

The house hadn't yet memorized my features or the family members, and it was still barren of blissful and sorrowful memories.

The war broke out while I was relocating to my new house with the help of my sister's children. I still remember, on the Friday night before the war, I called my driver's colleagues to bring the company vehicle on Saturday to move the rest of my furniture. They asked me to be patient until they got the director's approval. Saturday dawned, but I was forced to flee to the house that wasn't fully furnished. We spent the entire night listening to the thunder of shells and missiles—a counterpoint to the patriotic chants about the revolution and martyrs played on the radio.

So, my wife and I escaped again to my sister's house, which wasn't far away. She lived in the al-Nasr neighbourhood, next to the Friendship Sports Club. The area where both our houses were located was dangerous; the military sites of the resistance factions encircled us. We went to my sister's house, hoping the war would burn itself out within a week or two at most. But it carried on until the day I wrote this; we were unsure when there would be a ceasefire or what our fate would be.

The Occupation unleashed the most brutal assault across all the seven governorates of the Strip.

We stayed at my sister's for two days and one night. Missiles shredded the sanctity of homes. Children and women screamed, prayers soared, mosques were shuttered, street lights went out. Gaza was submerged in a swamp of blood. I remember, so clearly, the last night there. A loud voice made us tremble. My uncle and I ran into the street, asking what had happened.

'They're destroying the building close to ours. An officer from the intelligence called one of the residents, ordering us to evacuate immediately,' cried a young man running aimlessly, his voice etched in panic.

We left my sister's house and sprinted between the neighbouring buildings. I was looking for my children and my wife. 'Where did they go?' I asked. It was like doomsday in Gaza, as though all the people were called upon for judgement.

The building was not hit, despite the rumours that said otherwise. Anyway, we didn't return to my sister's house to this day; instead, we escaped to my sister's father-in-law's home, Uncle Moein al-Ghoul. We stayed up all night; the cacophony of ambulance sirens and horns of the civil defense vehicles tore at our souls and hearts. In the morning, my sister's husband came in after standing for hours just to secure half a bag of bread for breakfast. Even then, the Occupation targeted bread, water, and fuel lines. To think of eating became a crime, a transgression for which children, women, and even the defeated elderly paid the toll.

Again, we scattered. I returned to al-Shati camp, where my family lived, head bowed. We stayed for more than a month in my father's house. We carried gallons of water to wash away the stains of fear. After queuing to fill these gallons, my children dragged them in a cart for use in the camp's bathrooms and kitchens. Even there, we would hear the shelling, so we would run out to look for our children. Shreds everywhere. All camera lenses couldn't even capture the sheer scale of the tragedy. They bombed my cousin's house, Majed al-Ghoul. Sixty-four martyrs stepped out of the scene, most of them women. I climbed over the rubble in the morning, looking for their remains. But a cat arrived before me and devoured a piece of flesh. I wasn't sure if it was the flesh of my cousin's wife. His children? Or the displaced members of my big family, al-Ghoul?

That harsh period catalyzed resilience as we fathomed that more horrible things loomed ahead. We had to get ready for more death, more destruction, more thirst, more starvation. Just to let you know, we couldn't get water suitable for drinking. According to a UN report, the provided water was unsuitable for animal use. But even that water was scarce, as most water desalination plants had been targeted. We were forced to drink salty water from underground wells, water that could kill trees. What, then, could it do to a human being simply trying to survive?

My uncle, the children and I listened to the news while sitting on the balcony. The children's childhood was stolen. No more school, no more television. They aged years in the blink of an eye. Their thoughts and dreams grew big. They became experts at working under pressure, shouldering responsibility, and advocating for the rights of the Palestinians in the camp.

My son burst in, yelling, 'They're forcing us to the South…the south of Gaza Valley, towards Central Gaza, Khan Yunis, and Rafah.'

'Where can we go?' My mother shrugged.

'We won't get out even if they destroy the house over our heads,' my father said, his voice ringing with defiance.

We remained in the camp, as resilient as our neighbours, who were displaced daily, either individually or in groups, driven out by the unrelenting destruction and violence.

On the night of my fourth or perhaps fifth displacement, we stuck to our phones, listening to the news. In wars, phones are more than just for calls; they are torches and radios, enlightening the way to destiny. Suddenly, we heard deafening explosions that shook all the apartments. Windows were smashed. It was obvious that the shelling was so close. My brothers and I rushed outside to locate the bombing and help out the injured, clinging to the hope that someone, anyone, might have survived those deadly missiles weighing two pounds or more.

The al-Hessi family, the Halalo family, and others were bombed. The whole square was ablaze. We sprinted in all directions. Where could we look for the injured? It was dark, many were wounded, and the screaming was unbearable for our ears and hearts.

That morning, even those who were patient were confused. Where should we go? The South, too, was under siege—no safe shelter left for us. People wandered like haggard souls. We bumped into each other while heading towards the UNRWA schools, praying they might shield us from the shelling. Yet, recorded calls from an Intelligence Officer taunted us, proclaiming that there was no safe place in Northern Gaza. Were we truly meant to flee to the South? But where would we live? The number of people was immense. My wife and some neighbours urged me to go to the UNDP since the headquarters of this international organization was so close to al-Shifa Hospital. They couldn't assault it, as the UN flag was fluttering over it. We went there and stayed for two hours.

But we, then, felt suffocated. No bathrooms. Shared spots. Breaths intertwined, breeding a terrible psychological clash, suffocation, and heartache. What should we do? I, who had always prided myself on my strategic vision and constant planning for every move, was lost, adrift in this abyss, staring at people fighting over a metre of space here, over every room within those walls equipped with solar panels, electronic devices, and access to the Internet.

Then, out of the blue, my wife said, 'Yusri, I don't want to die here. Let's move to my family's house in Jabalia camp, in the al-Jurn area. It's much safer than Gaza and its camps. I want to die with my mother.'

Once again, we shouldered our luggage and bid farewell to my parents. We set off on an arduous journey on foot, starting from al-Shati camp. We made our way to the al-Rimal neighbourhood, then through the al-Nafaq region and the al-Sheikh Radwan neighbourhood. Finally, we headed towards the al-Jurn region in Jabalia. My mother-in-law, her sons, and the shelling were awaiting me. I stayed there for more than forty-five days, during which I was subjected to bombardment and sniping more than once.

But God's will ordained that I would be the most prominent one to bear witness to this plight that occurred in the North of the Gaza Strip, writing about hunger that invaded the city, dying for a handful of flour, walking through the alleys to grab a kilo of lentils, the quadcopters that killed people, drones still buzzing in my ear.

Yousri Alghoul, a Palestinian writer from al-Shati refugee camp in Gaza City, has endured Israel's attacks alongside his wife and four children. A passionate novelist, he was dedicated to nurturing young minds through literature. His personal library of 3,000 books, a cherished community space, was destroyed in an airstrike. Undeterred, he salvaged books from the rubble—his own and those of shattered schools. Despite losing friends, students, and his life's work, Yousri remains in Gaza, guiding children to channel their grief into writing. His latest novel, *Mashaniq al-'Atmah* (Gallows of Darkness), explores the perilous journeys of Palestinian and Syrian refugees to Europe.

My Dear Friend, Youssef
by Bahaa Shahera Rauf
Translated by Basma Nagy

My friend Youssef was martyred yesterday.

I didn't know our last call would be the day before his martyrdom. I didn't know that our banter, to distract from the enveloping smoke, about the rising price of cigarettes, would be our last.

Now, after calming down since I heard the news, I started laughing at all our inside jokes. I truly laughed a lot, after having cried a lot. Youssef was always the dividing line, the hair that separated us from not caring about how others were doing. He was very kind to us and to our hearts.

On the beach, one hot summer day, he had told me that he experienced racism from a young child because of his dark skin. I jokingly placed my hand next to his and told him, 'We're both dark, so now we're brothers.' That was a turning point in our friendship. We announced the birth of our brotherhood to the world, celebrating over a cup of bad coffee that was the colour of our skin, the birth of a genuine bond through which we would face this harsh and wearisome world together.

I never considered Youssef an ordinary friend. Rather, he was a friend when you were in need; a friend who knew how to comfort a tired heart until jasmine bloomed around it; an irreplaceable friend who made up for the many years of loneliness that preceded him.

Today, my heart is very heavy with his departure. I didn't know he carried this heavy load on my behalf. My loss is huge, equal to that of an orphan. I feel orphaned without you, Youssef, I swear.

I never expected to outlive him. I often asked him to save my suicide notes because I would not last long on this earth after him. The treacherous feeling is back, Youssef. The treason of living without you.

Youssef, my love. My love, Youssef. You will never die, I swear.

February 23, 2024

Bahaa Shahera Rauf is a Palestinian writer residing in Deir Al Balah near the historical site of Al Khidr. Along with a group of friends, he actively participates in assisting various places in Gaza. Ever since the war, Bahaa has been struggling with depression, but that hasn't stopped him from assisting the community as he feels he has a national duty to fulfil and a national struggle to follow through for the people. He exemplifies the steadfast spirit of the people of Gaza, as despite the fears and anxiety they carry about what's to come, they also have an inherent pride in their resilience and the strength of their thoughts and concepts.

Has Ouda Arrived?
Written and translated by Basman Eldirawi

My friends will meet in heaven,

and I'll look up at the sky and ask Issa:

Tell me, has Ouda arrived?

He jokes, *Haven't you heard his voice?*

Maybe I'll strike up a conversation, as always,

What does heaven look like?

Did you meet God?

Maybe now they're working together;

in the Gaza that Hiba saw under construction in the sky,

when they were down here—

before the war devoured our raw hearts,

burning whatever particles were left of the city.

They treat the martyrs whom the missiles left in their final forms, they work up there in the new Gaza:

in a hospital that's not threatened with destruction.

Then they sing, and they laugh, and they joke.

Hiba sits in a corner, writing a new poem,

and they cry in secret for their little ones

who remain orphans on Earth;

who know parents, but only in stories

and in the remains of photos,

the ones not destroyed by the occupier.

They ask God to protect them;

in their hearts is a fire that won't be put out.

They try to sleep but cannot;

although the night is quiet,

and

there are no bombs.

Basman Eldirawi is a 29-year-old physiotherapist and writer from Gaza. He graduated from Al-Azhar University in 2010 and has a deep love for films, music, and working with people with special needs. Since the war began in 2023, he has been documenting the experiences of Palestinians in Gaza, striving to bring their struggles to light.

Hello, This Is Ahmad from Gaza
by Ahmed Mortaja
Translated by Enas El-Torky

The thing I fear most is that my name will become a breaking news story, saying for example: 'X number of victims were recovered during heavy shelling on X area,' and I would become a dull number in the midst of all the countless numbers that haven't ceased until this moment. I don't want my name, and my family name, to be reduced to mere numbers, whether odd or even.

I have many dreams, for example: to travel outside the world of Gaza to a wider world, to explore it, to practice my language with others, and to truly believe that the scenes, images, and experiences I see online that show the world and its diversity, do exist.

I'm talking to you now, and I have no information about what's happening outside; I mean outside my home, where we returned after our neighbourhood was bombed a few days ago. There is no means of communicating with anyone, the sounds of shelling haven't stopped, and the flares are illuminating the area; warning of something unknown to us.

The thing I fear most is that everything will come to seem like normal events, and that it will become normal to bomb a house, and the abnormal thing would just be not giving a warning in advance. It will become normal for a child to die, whereas the abnormal thing would be that he died screaming, as well as many other things that can't be covered in a single text.

I'm Ahmad, and my friends call me Asim/Assoumi. By the way, I don't know the news of many of my friends. I check on them through short videos whenever I have the opportunity to be online. I check all the faces, make sure my friends aren't among them, but at the same time I realize that all those in the pictures and videos are my friends…so I cry.

I'm Ahmad, and since childhood, I've hated Arabic lessons and Arabic grammar. I hate the 'find the difference between two things' questions. I hate answers, and I love questions.

A couple of days ago, I was pondering the question, 'What's the difference between escalation and war?' And I wondered at the time what the significance of the question was as long as the outcome was the same: a mother crying, a child screaming. That is, if they get the chance to cry or scream.

I'm Ahmad, and I am afraid that I'll die and become an insignificant number, and that everything will be gone before I complete the text.

Ahmed Mortaja is a writer born in 1996 in Gaza City. He studied psychology and was actively involved in various cultural organizations in the city. With over seven years of experience as a psychologist for NGOs across the Gaza Strip, he dedicated his work to supporting others. Before the war, he could often be found enjoying pies on the beach with friends—but everything changed after October 2023. On October 28, he survived a bombardment that destroyed his home. Emerging from the rubble, he continued to write.

I Weep Only for Gaza
by Raed Shniowra
Translated by Nancy Roberts

When I was a little boy, I used to cry so easily that my mother would say to me, 'You've always got a tear on your cheek!' And it was true. I was extremely sentimental, and the slightest thing could bring tears to my eyes: a romantic or a sad scene in a movie, a moment of overwhelming joy, and even small triumphs, like when I got three stars on a homework assignment, or when some naive, awkward friend did something that made us split our sides laughing, or when I received a gift of money from an older relative on a holiday morning. And maybe I just cried because my heart was so full of life.

But in the summer of 2005, something happened that made my tears stop coming. I was overcome by a fit of weeping that went on for hours and hours, and I lost the ability to let the tears flow.

It was a July afternoon. I'd graduated from high school with honours, and my family and I were getting ready to leave Medina, the city where I'd been born, and move to Gaza. We were supposed to travel overland by bus from Medina to the Port of Aqaba in Jordan. From there, an Egyptian ocean liner would take us to Egypt's Nuweiba Port, after which we would go by car to the Rafah border crossing between Egypt and Palestine.

As I had done so many times in the past, I stood at the street corner near our house, next to a small grocery store where I'd made all sorts of memories. Then I went in for the last time to buy some snacks for the hours-long trip ahead. The store's owner, Abu Turki al-Hazimi, refused to take my money. He even tore up our page in the notebook where he kept a record of how much customers owed him if they'd had to buy something on credit, and cancelled all the debts we owed him. He lowered his glance, his eyes filled with tears.

My brothers and sisters started calling me, since it was time for us to get in the cars that would take us to the bus station. My cousin Mahmoud was standing next to me when all of a sudden, I burst into tears and collapsed, crying like a little boy whose only toy had been taken from him, or who had lost his mother and father at the same time, or maybe something worse. At that moment, I couldn't identify the reason for all this weeping. Whatever the reason was, I couldn't say goodbye to any of my friends, relatives or neighbours. With some difficulty, they picked me up and got me into the car, with me sobbing hysterically the entire time. I was still crying when we got to the bus station, where we would have to wait for an hour and a half until all the passengers had gathered and the luggage had been loaded onto the bus. Meanwhile, I kept crying nonstop. My mother, my siblings and my friends all tried to calm me down, but it was of no use.

We boarded the bus and it started on its way, while I sat in my seat doing nothing but sob. My tears were like a wild monsoon rain that seemed to never end. Nearly six hours into the 12-hour trek from Medina to Aqaba, my tears were still coming in a steady stream. Eventually, without knowing how, I dozed off out of sheer exhaustion, my heart paralysed with dread. I didn't sleep long, an hour at the most. In any case, I woke up to the sound of a song coming from somewhere. Amr Diab was singing, 'Don't worry, I haven't forgotten you!' My sister had opened up my bag and brought out a cassette tape of Amr Diab's greatest hits. And because just the night before, my poor heart had bidden farewell forever to its first love, I burst into tears all over again. Things went on this way until we crossed the Saudi–Jordanian border and pulled up in the Port of Aqaba.

The moment we arrived, my tears dried up, and that was that.

During my initial years in Gaza, I was a stranger to my own country. In my heart of hearts, I totally rejected the idea of staying there. Even in my worst nightmares, I would never have chosen to live in Gaza, the reason being that during my years as an expatriate in Saudi Arabia, I had been in deep crisis over my identity. My family is native to Gaza, from the ancient and venerable Hayy al-Zaytun neighbourhood, the oldest neighbourhood in the city. But as the days and years passed after moving back, it took possession of me too. I fell in love with it. I became attached to it, as though we belonged to each other. It was there that I went through my rebellious days, finished my university studies, and got my first job. It was there that I began to fulfil my dreams and most cherished ambitions, making friends who belonged to the same country, and so much more.

In spite of all the setbacks I suffered in Gaza, including long days and nights of loathing for everything in it, the wounds and defeats it caused me, including the loss of so many loved ones, moments of personal brokenness, pain, weariness and sorrow, and grinding wars that destroyed me on the inside, my tears refused to come. I used to tell the people closest to me, who were amazed at my ability to keep from crying even in the toughest moments, that I'd used up all my tears when I left Medina for Gaza.

The most difficult time of all for me, the time when I was most in need of my tears, may have been the day my father died in 2014. But even then, my tears let me down and stayed trapped in my heart as it held out in the face of what mountains themselves couldn't have endured.

Then came the blackest day of my entire life: Friday, October 13, 2023, just five days after 'the flood from hell' and the start of Israel's devastating war on the Gaza Strip. The occupation army had ordered the residents of Gaza City and the north of the Strip to evacuate the area and head south, beyond Wadi Gaza. After the Friday prayer, I set out with my wife and our little girls on the journey of endless pain, the journey away from Gaza.

We took a taxi from the Saraya Intersection to Rafah.

It might as well have been the Day of Ingathering and Resurrection. Thousands of people were lined up along the Saraya Intersection as entire families started making their way south. There was a torrential stream of people along the entire length of Jalaa Street, in addition to thousands more spread out on the ground, waiting for some means of transportation to take them south. But they were waiting in vain. I'd just been lucky. A driver who was also fleeing to Rafah happened to take pity on me and gave us a ride. The moment I got in the car and closed the door, my eyes erupted in tears. It was the same hysteria I'd experienced on the day I left Medina. The car went down Thalathini Street, then Ten Street, and on to Salah al-Din Street. The traffic was terrible, with some people on foot and others in cars, buses, and carts drawn by donkeys and horses. Everybody was heading south. But at that moment, all these details were lost on me. My tears had washed away all my concentration, drowning me in a black hole of sorrow. With everything in me, I knew that this road led in only one direction, and that I was saying goodbye to Gaza for good.

When we got to Kaff Miraj, in the area that separates the Khan Younis and Rafah governorates, my tear ducts shut off their valves once and for all. By the time we'd been in Rafah for just ten days, I couldn't endure being separated from the north one moment longer, and before the tanks could cut the north of the Strip off from the south, I went back to Gaza City. There I experienced the ground incursion into the city down to the last detail. With my own eyes, I watched the city dying, falling, being pulverized, ground to bits, marred beyond recognition as it was turned to rubble and dust, its blood spattering me in the face. But I didn't cry. My eyes didn't shed a single tear.

On the first of March, 2024, one day after the famed Nabulsi Roundabout massacre[3] on Gaza's sea coast, I was displaced once more from Gaza, and settled in Rafah until it too was overrun by the occupation army. Then I was displaced from Rafah to Nuseirat. And like all other Gazans who've lived through this grim year, a year in which they've lost everything: their homes, their families, their neighbourhoods, their neighbours, their streets, their sea, the city's coffee shops, its nighttime and its daytime, its laughter and its shouts, the loud bustle of its holidays and wedding celebrations, its ups and downs, my eyes haven't teared up once. My heart's dried up and hardened. I want to wring my eyes until the tears come gushing out and bury me in a watery grave because I've lost my Gaza forever, and I weep for her alone.

Raed Shniowra is a Palestinian journalist and poet from Gaza. He authored the poetry collection *I Loved Your Name on the Keyboard*. He has co-founded several initiatives and collectives aimed at revitalizing the cultural scene in Gaza.

---

[3] Also known as 'the flour massacre,' which took place on February 29, 2024, when at least 100 Palestinians were killed and 750 injured after Israeli forces opened fire on Palestinians seeking food from aid trucks on Gaza City's coastal Al-Rashid Street. The incident is opined to be the deadliest mass casualty event to have taken place in the Gaza Strip since Israel's onslaught on Gaza began in October 2023. Not long before this, the World Food Programme had reported that more than half a million Palestinians in Gaza were at risk of famine.

...Beside the River
by Husam Maarouf
Translated by Soha El-Sebaie

We no longer want anything from you.

Your lifeless gaze

won't stretch far enough to bring us peace.

You are out of the frame, and the storm won't calm today.

Move your eyes, shut them,

shed tears,

in this furious air, you can swim forever,

but the one looking through the spyglass doesn't save the drowning man.

We no longer want anything from you,

your loud voices

won't lift our screams to the heavens.

That image that pains you:

those are your disappointments at getting nowhere.

As for the amputated hand that pierces your gaze,

that's your eternal sorrow…maybe you've seen it among the carnage.

That hungry belly,

is the space between you and life.

No use crying beside the river twice;

the first causes a wave,

the second wipes it away;

it's the river, a continuation of the void.

The violated body offers no exercise in pity,

shock does not require feet, but rather wings to fly.

The laugh that comes at the moment of death is perhaps not merely a movement of the lips,

and do we know why the hungry man laughs?

Reassured, as if he'd seen a cat take a bite of his future corpse.

We no longer want a thing from you…

Only to die in safety.

March 1, 2024

Husam Maarof is a poet and editor who is actively involved in Gaza's literary scene. He is the co-founder of the youth assembly 'Utopia for Knowledge'. He was awarded the Mahmoud Darwish Museum Prize for prose poetry (2015) and the Badr Al-Turki Foundation for Cultural Development Prize (2015), for his poetry collection *The Scent of Glass to Death,* and released his debut novel *Izmeel Ram* in 2020, published by Al-Ra'at and Bridges of Culture Publishing House. Before the war, Husam wrote on Facebook only short verses of poetry. He is currently in Gaza.

Small Window into Gaza: 'What Did They Do to Your Eyes, Yousif?'

by Mohammed Al-Zaqzooq

Translated by Luke Leafgren

> *I came to you from there*
> *At the end of the year*
> *The year of endings*
>
> —Sargon Boulus, 'Gods of the Bitter Zaqqum'

It didn't occur to me when I heard the poem, 'Gods of the Bitter Zaqqum,' by Sargon Boulus, an Iraqi, that this would be the Arabic poem that was the truest, the most precise, and the smartest poem that embodied the reality of life in Gaza during the war that has been raging since October of last year.

The first chance I had, I listened to it again with a good Internet connection so it could play through at full speed without any buffer.

'My god! What a coincidence,' I said. 'That's saying exactly what I want to say.' I specifically wanted to listen to the poem, not read it. The rhythm of the words has music. You feel it, you almost see it, and it translates the mixed feelings contained within the poem: despair, followed by a question, then a scream, and finally, indifference.

Somehow, the text and its music shook loose the boulder of ossified emotions that were weighing upon my soul, binding me in shackles of fear, anxiety, displacement, and astonishment. There was no sadness, just a massive stone at the base of the soul, which the words of the poem began rolling until it arrived at sadness. The sadness was warm and deep. It moved like a secret, like the sound of whispers, deep in the folds of the body, and then came crashing down in the form of tears.

> *What did they do to your eyes, Yousif?*
> *What did they do to your eyes? Oh, God!*
>
> —Sargon Boulus, 'Gods of the Bitter Zaqqum'

I happened to see my face in a mirror placed in the corner of a small alley with a large collection of tents for the uprooted. It was a pale face, a yellowish face, it had two eyes exactly as Sargon Boulos describes them: extinguished, as though something had stolen their light.

Stunned, I couldn't take another step. At that moment, I felt unable to move my feet, but the people pushing among the tent alleys of the displaced in the Mawasy district of Khan Younis forced me to keep walking, leaving behind the shock of seeing the mirror reflect a face that seemed to belong to someone else.

I hadn't seen my face at all since the time I left my house, uprooted for the first time. After all, there were no mirrors in the tents. And it really didn't matter to me, nor to many others. A mirror isn't the kind of thing you pack when being driven from your home. I had looked at my face once before leaving the house. What shone back at me in the mirror was nothing to write home about, even though, even then, I had not yet had the experience of being uprooted.

What I saw now was a pale face, a yellowish face, with a big, black circle drooping under each eye. On either side, running parallel to the nose, was an arched line that disappeared among all the other lines when any expression came over the face, only to reappear clearly when my face became still once again.

Additional lines appeared on the forehead above the face. I particularly noticed those as, before the war, I had always been aware of them and carefully monitored their existence. As for the rest of the body, it was suffering from emaciation and a marked loss of weight.

After a few weeks, I saw this face again in the eyes of others. We were three friends who had not been able to meet for more than five months. The displacement had scattered us across a landscape that was new to us, now that clusters of tents clothed the whole Gazan coast in new forms, narrow and choked. And so, the opportunities to meet were much restricted, and when we saw each other for the first time after a separation of over five months, each of us felt a certain sense of embarrassment towards the others, feelings both foolish and painful of wanting to curl up and disappear. It was as though each of us wanted to escape the grim signs we saw.

Each of the three faces summed up the war—the blaze of the sun, the frustration of waiting, the hardship of trudging over rugged roads, emaciation, fear, and many, many other things—and it pained each of us to be seen in that way by the others. But after a few heavy minutes that felt like a lifetime, we were able to get past that emotion with a mixture of consoling phrases and some jokes.

We made our way through surging crowds of the dispossessed, trying to find any place we might sit and talk. There was a scale by the side of the road, a large one, the kind used for weighing goods. Some uprooted person, trying to find a way to earn some money, had set it alongside the road, with a small handwritten cardboard sign that said, 'Know your weight for only one shekel.'

Month after month of war, after the acute crisis in the food supply, in addition to the gruelling daily exertions that people undertook to acquire water for washing and drinking, countless kilometres traversed by foot, and so many other tedious and exhausting aspects of daily life, everyone had lost a great deal of weight. So, someone decided that placing a scale on the roadside would be a good idea, and many people might want to know how many kilograms they had lost over those months.

The scale provoked curiosity in all three of us, and one after another, we took turns standing on it. We were surprised to learn how much of our bodies we had lost over just a few months. The least amount of weight lost by any of us was fifteen kilograms. We were stunned: that much weight could hardly be lost if we had gone on a hunger strike. We burst into bitter laughter, making fun of all the modern diets and weight loss methods, for there was no system more effective than ours. A war like this was all it took to produce miracles.

It was the nights of bombardment, the fear tremors, heart poundings, hands trembling, the whisperers roaming your head, the waves of sadness and depression that repeatedly stretched the nerves; it was burning in the sun's searing rays while standing in lines, scenes of destruction, the smell of gunpowder, the sound of explosions, and many, many other things that did their work and left their marks on the body and the face. While the marks they made in the consciousness, the emotions, and the soul remained more cruel and painful, even if the body hid them behind skin and bones and blood vessels.

Whenever I looked at the faces of those passing by, in vehicles or among the tents, I saw dying faces.

What has happened? I said to myself. These faces are dying. My god! They are dying faces. Eaten by the sun. Sapped by depression. Twitching features that grimaced at the traumatic horror and the awfulness of what was happening, while pains and questions piled up within them.

Faces bearing dense pain, contracted and concentrated, dumped there by past days. And a dominating fear that envelops the present. Endless apprehensions and misgivings, the expectation of worse things to come.

Endless murmurs and thoughts circled in my head about dying faces in living bodies that moved amid shattered scenes of devastation. These are the faces of people in Gaza. Whenever we ask how they are doing, they say they're fine. A quick, mechanical reply; the falseness of which is revealed by the first glance that smashes into their dead faces.

And when I made my way along the roads, it was so hard for me to recognize the faces of friends I knew from my years at school and work, now that war had carved their faces, as though hewing stones, with chisels of fear and deprivation and loss. Some of them tried to avoid being seen, walking with the same dead face and trying to get away from chance encounters that might reveal the magnitude of suffering they had endured in just a few months. Others went past without me even being able to recognize them.

Dying faces, bleary eyes, bony bodies after serious loss and malnutrition, dirty clothes, feet dusty and cracked by the obdurate road. People wandering in a crowd among tents on a futile, miserable course that runs in empty circles of suffering and deprivation, driven from one place to another by falling shells.

What hell is this? Such a hell.

Mohammed Al-Zaqzooq is a researcher born in Khan Younis in 1990. He studied Arabic language and literature at Al-Aqsa University and is a contributor to various Palestinian and Arab platforms. Mohammed is an active member in literary and cultural organizations shaping Gaza's cultural landscape and the former general coordinator of the 'Utopia for Knowledge' assembly. Currently, he coordinates community library and youth teams at the Tamer Foundation for Community Education. His poetry collection *The Soothsayers of Khanun* won the Khalili Poetry Award at the First Palestinian Cultural Forum for Creative Writers in 2018. Mohammed has ardently worked alongside Mahmoud to bring all the poets and writers together to aid this collection. Despite the challenges with communication, he has consolidated the most authentic and heart wrenching writings which can bring us somewhat closer to understanding the emotional and physical toll of this horrific time.

A Soul as Vast as the Universe
by Hiba Abu Nada
Translated by Nihal Shafik

If you think I have remembered you,
even once,
know that I have forgotten you
a thousand times in this poem.

In the prolonged sound of silence,
where the senses fail to find
their voice and sight,

and there:

in the hut of absence,
on the bristles of the shivering mat

in the room of forgetfulness,
where the sun never reaches
the rust of the beds

upon the waterwheels,
standing above the rivers
of endless fading

as if they had wiped out the palm groves,
leaving nothing in the abyss
but the soul of a date

a flood of names flowed
under my pen,
like a drop
none of them lingered on it.

The meadows are full of longing roses;
yet they shimmer not for a second,
nor did a filly
neigh for you.

I walk the paths of the absent;
yet I do not seek you there
not even if I stumbled.

In the street of affection, never
do memories extend a hand
for water or a scrap.

The bread of words there has grown stale;
and love, in the shadow of memory,
appears tenfold.

I stripped my memory bare
and began to weave, from the start,
a vest for the child's heart.

I shed the henna of longing,
and with my own hands
I'll birth tomorrow's light.

As my wounds ripened into awe,
and the flowers, to me, turned to embers,
of pure redness.

As I have grown with them fully,
no smallest dream remains
within my soul, vast as the universe.

As my mind has come to realize
the sacredness of its own being,
it will no longer even consider
finding its own answers.

I don't make sweets to forget,
bitter food wields more power,
and the poem remains bitter.

This is because my prophecy foretold:
I will comprehend the wisdom of clay,
and will not weep for a shattered jar.

My back—I do not claim you broke it—
yet something in you sought to break it.
My wings, once burdened with pain,
now fly freely
in the skies of might.

Hiba Abu Nada was a Palestinian novelist, poet, educator, and nutritionist from Gaza. Her novel *Oxygen is Not for the Dead* won the Sharjah Award for Arab Creativity in 2017. She held a BA in Biochemistry and an MA in Clinical Nutrition from the Islamic University. Hiba was killed alongside her son in October 2023 by the Israeli bombardments.

All of This—Why?

by Mahmoud Jouda

Translated by Enas El-Torky

Calm, unusually. The sky was free from flying iron, and the moon scattered its light over a prodigious collection of tents in Rafah. One of these tents was lit from within, giving it the appearance of a large star, albeit an earthbound one. From outside, a radio could be heard; its owner seemed to be searching for a news station to confirm the rumour of a ceasefire. After a long expedition over the radio dial with no real news, the person's fingers halted on a station that was broadcasting Um Kulthoum's song *This Is My Night*. Shortly afterwards, the tent's light dimmed. It appeared that the battery had run out and the man had fallen asleep.

People here sing. Song is by no means synonymous with joy; people haven't stopped repeating the pieces they know so well.

Early one morning, displaced people in the camp woke to a scorching sunshine that was unusual for these wintry nights. I heard a voice, one of the girls singing a song of Shadia's: *Tell the sun not to blaze so bright, my darling is leaving in the morning.*

I didn't notice anyone walking in the street, in the sunshine—perhaps Darling was walking somewhere else, looking for flour or rice, or maybe he was in a detention queue. The crucial thing was that Darling was still upright, walking on both feet.

Another song sent me on a long, wandering walk. A small wedding between the tents, a girl of surpassing beauty; if the circumstances had been otherwise I would have thought her in her fourth year of university. She was opening the hand of the young groom and kissing it as she sang: *He closed his eyes and held out his hand for henna.* She put henna on his palm and closed his fingers over it.

This is what we might term forlorn joy.

On another dumping ground, an elderly woman with a green tattoo on her chin was stroking her shrouded husband's face as he lay on the pavement, and she was wailing the same song: *He closed his eyes.* We sing this song at weddings and funerals here, I don't know why. It is a deep Palestinian secret.

On Sea Street (I love this name very much, although the municipality insisted on naming it after the Caliph of the Faithful) the man came walking, clearly distracted; he kept colliding with passersby and the goods of the new traders in the middle of the street, a road no longer wide enough for a song. The whisper of it came to me through the man's soft crooning as I drew parallel to him: *All of this—why?*

People still sing, and I still walk in the streets, shuffling in my mother's slippers, continually in song. Because, as Victor Hugo said, 'When hope is gone, song remains.'

February 27, 2024

Mahmoud Jouda is a young writer from Gaza. He lived there with his two daughters. He has authored *Orphan Gaza, Letters to Baghdad,* and *Garden of Legs*. He continues to document the reality of the war through his words. He is currently trying to move out of Gaza for the safety and future stability of his two young girls.

My Memory Is Proficient at Paining Me
by Mayar Nateel
Translated by Enas El-Torky

'Good morning, beautiful.' This is how I used to wake up at dawn to prepare for my normal day, to the voice of Fairuz and a cup of mint tea, and sit in the balcony for half an hour watching the neighbourhood children leave for school, with the sea in front of me, and the sounds of gulls and crows rising as the waves crash.

The city streets surprise my heart with their stillness, and the light movement of cars and buses, from Al-Karama Street to Bahloul Station, where everyone takes off to head to university or work, and Nasr Street, where people stop at Al-Khouli Bakery to buy pastries for breakfast and continue their way with the rhythm of the streets and cafes.

University Road bustles with students and graduates. Every two steps, you find one of your classmates from elementary or middle school, or you find an old friend that you lost track of for a while. Between one university and another, you find a falafel shop with a queue of male and female students awaiting their turn, and Samir Mansour's bookshop that is packed with people browsing, as well as university offices with their share of students, isolating themselves away from the noise of lectures.

Nothing separates University Road from the sea and the port of Gaza except for some conversations with a friend like Nour, who is good at listening, two cups of coffee, the warm winter sun, and the breeze caressing my hair. The sea knows how to take your weary words and rearrange them and enable you to complete your day normally.

From there, your feet take you to an art exhibition at the French Cultural Centre at the Ansar roundabout, where there is a cultural café where you meet some friends who are adept at using words to illustrate the painting hanging on the wall, and are skilled at writing texts to fascinate you with the ecstasy of novice lovers' suffering in a city bustling with mundane life and confusion.

In Gaza, we adore going for walks. You'll find us walking from Al-Abbas intersection to Rashad Al-Shawa to attend a social seminar or enjoy the taste of nabulsi kanafeh from 'Abu Saud'. We continue walking to the streets of Al-Rimal and Omar Al-Mukhtar, where we buy some ice cream from 'Kazem' and find the kiddie cars in the middle of the Unknown Soldier's square, and the balloon vendors, that children cry over, and cotton candy vendors, and the delicious taste of corn sprinkled with paprika from the Saraya intersection. The route is endless, and the day doesn't end simply like this.

From Al-Rimal to the Palestine Stadium, and a meeting with the Yara'at youth team, and some iced coffee from the 'We'll Remain Here' café. In front of you, you'll find 'the tree of cities' as you measure the distance between you and your city of origin, being a refugee. At the Yara'at meeting, discussion in the auditorium doesn't pause about Ghassan Kanafani and Mahmoud Darwish, and friends don't cease writing the time and place. Our friend Haider stands up to silence us with his words so that we may call him our poet, and Muhammad Sami surprises us with his voice and may sing for us. There are papers, thoughts, and the delicious flavour of tea from Basma's hands.

The day doesn't end, and I don't stop drowning in its pleasures. I love my home, and I love the road leading to it. I sing with the breeze in the street, as my hair flutters. I buy some bread from Al-

Yazji Bakery, a sesame cake, and qrashel[4], to be eaten with tea. A flora tree embraces the house, the keys of which I can never leave without, whereas my sister manages to forget them every time. Chickens scatter in the courtyard of the house where the sage and basil grow, alongside the roses that my father waters daily.

In the evening, I get myself ready once again for another stroll by the sea, but this time with the family. We head to Al-Sudaniya beach, strolling along the illuminated night streets, as the earth rejoices in the absence of the sun's heat, and Umm Kulthum's voice rings along the Corniche cafes. The night wipes the fatigue of the day, and the sea washes away the insomnia of the night to ease sleep.

A bed and a pillow; these things are mine alone, as well as a closet against the wall, containing everything I chose to buy: perfumes, creams, and clothes. I'm competent at caring for the house and all its furniture. I don't like dust settling on it, and I like to see guests impressed with the shining bookshelves, and to rearrange the house after children leave.

I'm skilled at remembering my days, and the city streets. I'm proficient at painting my wonder with it every morning, as if I don't know it, as if I'm seeing its streets for the first time. I may be good at hugging friends, not good at forgetting their names, good at memorizing their faces and their finest outfits. I'm good at memorizing the kitchen shelves, all the utensils, and the fastest way to prepare pasta salad.

I remember two years ago I was visiting Deir al-Balah in August for training, and I would end the day with a karak tea from Paparotti's café. I have no relatives in the south, so I'm not used to being there for more than ten months, and I didn't prepare myself for this.

For three hundred days and more, I've been training my memory to remember the streets, as I walk through southern Gaza. I remember the first day I came to the south, I remember how I left my pillow

---

[4] Moroccan sesame rolls.

on my bed and didn't think of taking it, and didn't take a bag containing the streets or cafes.

The war stubbornly takes away my home and the road leading to it, stubbornly makes me get used to a home that isn't mine, forces me to adapt to the tent and its heat. The war defies me, and I defy it with my refusal, so it turns my warm home into rubble. The war stubbornly robs me of friends or their laughter. Between the diaspora and checkpoints, between the coffins and the grief of loss, I mourn them. There are no cafes here in the south with the conversations of my friends, and no sea to hold their gaze, and carry me away from the war.

I defy the war, and it defies me back by cutting communication networks, or cutting out lives. 'Hello, Wisam. Let me know how you're doing. Tell me you haven't become a fleeting statistic in the minds of the world.'

The war defies me and paralyses me. All the streets have been razed, all the places have been swallowed by the earth, and the distance separating me and my university graduation project is now greater than my age. Joy has become too small to announce the birth of a new baby after seven barren years, so we hide our joy and limit it to a call—the first half of which is congratulations, and the second half is mourning for those who have gone.

I don't know how to be stubborn anymore. Oh God, I'm trying. I'm trying not to be devoured by missile shrapnel, or the darkness of the siege. I'm trying to survive with the two shirts that I remembered to flee our house with. I'm trying to survive with an intact body, not consumed by hunger, while my aunt's body there is devoured by hunger on a daily basis.

I'm adept at defeat in the face of disappointments, so the radio announcer kills me with news of the end of negotiations, prolonging the war. I'm defeated daily in face of Death, as it stubbornly leaves me to the War to torture me more. I'm defeated by sleeping on the floor, without hovering over my bed at home. I'm defeated by the cold water that washes my body once a week, by the winter cold, without a blanket and windows. I've been defeated by the shrapnel.

I don't know how to arrange my words in the face of my defeat, so I let an earthen mattress embrace my exhausted body, let the sky blow the dust out of my eyes, and the cawing of crows wash the sounds of war from my ears. I'm skilled at pitching a tent and breaking my hunger with a loaf of bread and some za'atar and hugging my mother when Death looms over us.

I'm not bargaining over my displacement, I'm not negotiating with the world for an announcement that precedes the news of my martyrdom, but I'm afraid I'll be blown to bits, and my father won't be able to collect my remains in a black bag. I'm afraid that I'll wake up tomorrow remembering how I used to spend my normal day listening to the voice of Fairuz at Al-Sudaniya beach, as I pack my bags for yet another exodus.

Mayar Nateel is a writer from Gaza and a talented 23-year-old artist. She recently graduated with a degree in English literature from the Faculty of Arts and Humanities at Al-Aqsa University in Gaza. Mayar has a large, artistic family. Their home, once filled with their father's artwork, has been destroyed, as has her brother's home. They have 'narrowly escaped death several times'. Despite these ongoing challenges, her sister has not given up on her dreams and still hopes to write her first novel.

Salt Lakes

by Hind Joudah

Translated by the ArabLit Collective

Sorrow is the gift given to us by the world,

we are its eternal children who never grow old!

Our unique sadness comes in many forms, as if it fears leaving us bored:

an explosion may hit the roof,

or it can tear up the asphalt on the ground, its trees, its graveyards.

It might come in the form of a blind or a dud shell,

or prevent food from reaching us until our bellies tremble from the dreaded sound of its void.

For too long, we shed tears.

We cried for a long time to earn these gifts,

and they came again in the shape of a tent!

Dear world,

In short, we are the culmination of your deep and brutal grief.

We are your salt lakes.

February 25, 2024

Hind Joudah is a poet from Al-Breij Refugee Camp, Gaza. She has published two collections of poems titled *Someone Always Leaves* and *No Sugar in the City*. Before the war she also worked in radio production, and with Workers Radio in Gaza. She produced and presented a show called *Good Morning, Homeland* for Radio Al-Hurriya in Gaza. She won the Appreciation Prize by the Youth Ideas Association for her short story, and the Golden Prize at the Arab Youth Gathering Festival in Cairo in 2006. Her writings were received in November 2023.

TELL THE SUN
NOT TO
BLAZE SO BRIGHT

Christmas Eve
by Batool Abu Akleen
Translated by Ibrahim Fawzy

Like a wolf that
lost its pack,
so fear shredded its huge body,
tore out its fangs,
gnashed its claws.
Just like this wolf,
I'm alone,
climbing the hills of days
where joy hasn't snowed this year.

I howl.
A family—warmed by a fire
burnt by the wooden-like corpses—
hears me.
The family opens gifts—
coated in the corpses' blood,
wrapped in the corpses' skin.
The family gulps wine to get drunk,
so not to hear my wailing.
The family double-checks the barred gates.
Laughter rings out.
I howl again
but with greater pain.

Just like that wolf,
I'm alone
on the abyss of pain, a volcanic crater.
Longing like lava melts me slowly,
cuts off my death,
melts my guillotine.
Each time my soul dissolves in its throes,
it's replaced with another one in greater pain.

Batool Abu Akleen is a poet and translator from Gaza, Palestine. She started writing at the age of ten, and at the age of fifteen, she won the Barjeel Poetry Prize for her poem 'It Wasn't Me Who Stole the Cloud,' which was published in the Beirut-based magazine *Rusted Radishes* and later included in the Italian anthology *Of Water and Time*. Akleen's poetry has been translated into several languages, including English and Italian, and featured in numerous international publications.

The Final Call
by Doha Kahlout
Translated by Haytham el-Wardany

Three months ago, the words 'I want to go to the South' were a difficult matter, accepted only after several attempts. I visited my friend quickly, returning home before sunset so my mother wouldn't worry. On the seventh day of the war, I heard my mother's voice calling, for the first time, 'We want to go to the South.' Words that interrupted my mind's wandering. Fear lined all our faces—my family's and my uncle's, his sons and their wives, and my sister with her husband and his family—when our helpless eyes met, and we understood without words that we were all wondering: 'Where can we go?'

The morning of the first Friday of the war, talk of seeking refuge south of the Wadi spread like wildfire. We gathered on the balcony of our house, watching in amazement as the queues of homes were loaded onto the backs of cars and trucks, and we repeated, 'We aren't going, where would we go?'

Within minutes, we felt as though the sounds were tearing out our hearts, and instantly the conversation changed into *we will go*, and each of us tried to find somewhere that would accommodate us all.

We had to say goodbye to our house, its rooms, and the details known only to its owner. But we imagined that, in this moment, you could either say goodbye to your memories or become a memory. I left the house without a look to fill my heart and mind.

Even now, I don't remember how we got from the house to the kindergarten that functioned as a shelter for displaced people. My last memory of the house is my mother's call that we must leave and go South.

What should you know?

You are the one who possessed the keys of life, and with your covetous hands, you paved all paths and took your first step towards a dream that envelops you as you envelop it. In a moment, you found yourself devoid of everything except fear: no work, no friends, no colleagues estranged from one another who only smile goodbye at the end of the day, no complicated tasks that you celebrate completing.

Falling into a void you imagine is a dream, you examine your memories from the left and the right, afraid that their long stagnation will rot them.

The first week of our migration, denial dominated my words and actions, and I slept and woke up in anticipation of the day of our return. I knew nothing of the outside world, and my friends knew very little of me. After a few days, I had to get used to it. I went out to see faces I didn't know who shared the center with us and—one way or another—I had to deal with strangers and share moments of their day.

Before the seventh of October, I would call any gathering of unknown people a 'crowd' and flee the scene. I knew that things had become difficult. It was difficult buying anything you might want to buy, everything I wanted to make would inevitably be lacking something that wasn't available, and in order to return victorious you had to engage in a struggle for a few loaves of bread. After a few days, we all knew that this place would take many days from our lives.

We understood and we learnt what had never occurred to us.

In order to survive, you must know how to seize opportunities, to overcome the fatigue of your feet, to ignore your rough, black hands, and to exhale the black smoke from your lungs. You must know all the ways to keep yourself and your child from getting sick, and if you are injured, you must know how to treat it without disturbing your neighbour—who's just lost his brother—with your trivial pain!

And you must now know, necessarily, your role in obtaining fresh water in order to survive.

January 17, 2024

Doha Kahlout is a poet and teacher from Gaza. Her first collection of poems, *Ashbah* (Similarities), was published in 2018. She was selected for a residency at Reid Hall in Paris as part of the Displaced Artists Initiative, co-sponsored by the Columbia Global Center and the Institute for Ideas and Imagination, but has not been able to take up her place since the Israeli invasion of Rafah and the closure of its border crossing in May 2024. She is currently in Deir al-Balah in central Gaza strip, from where she has been sharing her writings.

May I Write?
by Ahmed Mortaja
Translated by Enas El-Torky

It's close to 4 a.m. My decision not to write after the first day of the year proved unfair to myself. I can't see any reason not to write except that the boredom is killing me, and I don't have any other way.

This, amid the showers of bullets and bombs, is a good opportunity for me to curse the world for being so selective in its choice of issues, as part of its brief to monitor and evaluate killing methods, and its choice of the most humane and least bloody ways of ending our lives.

Then there's the fear. Our fear now centers on inventing ways other than screaming for the kids to express their fear, because screaming means you're alive, and that's a dangerous coincidence that is undesirable to the other side.

The other fear is about how to meet our and the children's food and drink needs. So many questions swirl around this fear, though I deliberately won't raise them here, dear reader, so as to allow you to imagine them for yourself. Oh, how I miss imagination.

It's now 4.30 a.m. This text took me two minutes to write; I spent the rest of the time holding my breath so as not to bother you while expressing my fear and my fatigue.

Good night.

January 29, 2024

Ahmed Mortaja is a writer born in 1996 in Gaza City. He studied psychology and was actively involved in various cultural organizations in the city. With over seven years of experience as a psychologist for NGOs across the Gaza Strip, he dedicated his work to supporting others. Before the war, he could often be found enjoying pies on the beach with friends—but everything changed after October 2023. On October 28, he survived a bombardment that destroyed his home. Emerging from the rubble, he continued to write.

Where…?

by Fida Abu Maryam

Translated by Mervat Youssef and Enas El-Torky

We left our home by itself—with a picture of my mom, the sounds of our songs, a cup of coffee on the table, a wedding photo, windows through which we watched the sea, unanswered questions about the odds of survival, the aroma of morning scents, secrets entrusted to pillows, fingerprints on kitchen knives, and scars of housework injuries.

The question seemed very minute at that moment, amongst all that we left behind, and all the questions converged into one: '*Where should we go?*'

A question that suits a small family wanting to escape the gaping jaws of a deadly murderous beast. We left our home by itself, seeing that the bags we evacuated with were too small to contain it.

There, in the house of my nana, who passed away six months before the war, grief still strikes the heart. She herself is the protagonist of the story of 'the eight-year-old girl', which she narrated every time we sought refuge in her home.

She recounted how her father took them and fled their home with them sixty or seventy years ago. Years drift away from us. Time is irrelevant; what matters is that she memorized the face of her fear while on her dad's shoulder who was carrying her to safety.

At that time, no one thought that war would create distances between homes—distances of barricades, soldiers, countries, tanks, jets, barbed wire, snipers, and murder, for all, ever since.

She has an amazing ability to remember all the moments, as well as that single question that sprung by the door of our house, in the face of all the other overwhelming questions:

'Where should we go?!'

It was the same one with no clear distinct answer.

'Where the wind is.' This works. Let it be the answer.

The wind might carry the memory of pain and depart.

The wind that might take the alternate house, 'the tent', and destroy it.

The wind whose howl might drown out the sound of wailing and farewell.

I left my lonely home, for the home of my nana, the protagonist of the story. She died and bequeathed us the conviction of eternal resistance. Whenever she saw an Arab congregation, she said:

'Had each one spit on the tyrant, it would have drowned.'

We would laugh at the naiveté of her proposition, only for her to continue, 'Walla, even a spit is too much.'

She approached the aftermath with the way of thinking of an eight-year-old girl who was carried by her father to a house where there is no killing or death but rather starvation and homelessness. As if one death is easier than another.

Hence started the Palestinian's relationship with death!

We survived in the house for a month or so, and the question transformed into a mountain.

'Where should we go' exceeded the ability of a small family and consumed more families.

From November 2023 to May 2024, I moved between five houses.

During that time, the question used to hide inside bags or slip away for a while, before returning to dart in front of the rooms of these houses or in their courtyards where I sat.

'*Where should we go?*'

I wish there was a spit, nana!

Until now, I have moved between houses that hosted me as a displaced person. Homes and their people opened their doors and arms wide open, receiving me and making it possible for me to survive with them.

All the homes resemble mine.

Each time we departed, they were left alone with photos, teacups, impressions of tales, secrets and fingerprints on kitchen knives, and a table and the impact of a long silence preceding a question:

'Where should we go?!'

The question weighed heavier than grief in a tale of a hero's defeat.

The question weighed heavier than grief after loss.

The question weighed heavier than silence after an explosion.

The question grows bigger and wider as it passes from hand to hand.

And for the first time, my nana's father's shoulder seemed to be the answer!

'Where should we go?!'

Narrating the tale or performing it commences thereafter.

The Palestinian is born subsequently to tell the tale and to leave the houses standing alone.

As he stands at their doors asking:

'Where should we go?!'

The Palestinian leaves the alternate houses all alone with an impression and a trace, a voice and a song, and fingerprints and photos.

I am now thinking of the finish line for the image of the shoulder that carried my nana at the end of the tale, if it ever takes place.

The departed return
The displaced
The wanderers
The lost
The yearning
The missing
The dispersed
The fearful
The buried
The newborns

They stand at the house door and release a collective sigh saying:

'*We know where to go.*'

This cry would serve as a reassuring ending to a tale of a diaspora and an ongoing Nakba, during which the question started out small, then became heavy, then we found the answer, and were confronted with the biggest question of all: 'When will all this happen?!'

A simple dream whose features appeared one day in 1948, in the sleep of an eight-year-old girl, and is still growing and narrowing, being uprooted and killed, sprouting and returning, blooming and withering, jumping and laughing, grieving, and suffering amputation, displacement, expulsion, and despite all still continues to be dreamt.

Returning to the home that we left all by itself, with everything that the bundles and bags could not carry.

Fida Abu Maryam is a Palestinian writer, educator, and cultural activist from Gaza. She is a founding member of the Utopia Initiative and has participated in numerous local and regional cultural events.

I Tread on Clouds
by Omer Hhammash
Translated by the ArabLit Collective

I was there.

Was I real, or a dream treading on clouds? Was I flesh and blood, or an illusion—a mirage?

I stepped on a cotton fleece; crowds upon crowds flooded in, their hands thick as forests, tearing at a screaming loaf of bread.

I descended, watching, or perhaps the clouds lowered me, into the dense and crippled hunger.

I escaped, only to soar again. I noticed the pilots' awe, though they paid me no heed. I heard passing laughter and the screech of iron close by; below me stood rubble, ceilings barely elevated, only to plummet, letting loose infernal boxes.

I fell, or nearly did. The crowd crumbled, the shreds of bread dipped in blood. I saw how dreams are torn apart before death, how a corpse's final act is to blossom—then wither, releasing its hold, so the dream takes flight.

I once thought dreams could breathe, and it came true. I beheld them as doves before they assumed their dove-like features, dreams that trampled the very legs of those who dreamed them.

I was there, uncertain if it was me, or my wandering dream.

February 4, 2024

Omer Hhammash is a Palestinian short story and novel writer born in 1953 in Gaza's refugee camps, where he resides. He co-founded the Palestinian Writers Union and published seven short story collections, two novels, and contributed to two Arabic short story anthologies. Some of his works were translated into English, Italian, and Hebrew. Omer was awarded the Palestine Appreciation Prize for 2024.

He Doesn't Know How This Week Has Passed
by Haidar al-Ghazali
Translated by Ibrahim Fawzy

He woke up early, as usual. Those moments are his; he owns and shapes the world as he wishes. It's Saturday, the day his weekly heartache is due. He recognizes that his holiday and outings with friends are over. He geared up for his class, beginning at eight in the morning with a short grammar quiz. He then drowned in a cacophony of vendors' voices. A sound from outside seemed familiar; it soared through the air, but unlike the chirping of sparrows.

Several homemade missiles came out from all directions. Something in this world wasn't as he wanted it to be. Hours later, he realized what was going on and was trapped in a question that he refused to answer, 'How will the enemy respond?'

Out of the blue, his father asked him to buy some bread. He went to the bakery, but it was empty. The grocer offered bags of flour at a high price, so not a single person bought flour.

In the evening, his family gathered in the living room, all under one roof, squeezing themselves in one seat. Still, American missiles halt only over children's heads.

He doesn't grasp the metamorphosis of time during the war, nor how each second he lives amidst the shelling stretches into an infinite lifetime. He doesn't know how they age each moment their little sister screams in terror when there's a nearby explosion.

If he didn't love the night when love dwells—its stars, tunes, and staying up late—he wouldn't gather in one room, laughing, worrying, weeping, waiting for a harrowing death, dreaming of dying together. When fire belts bombard their hearts, time stops for a brief moment. He grasps for the suffocating air to breathe in. But his life slips away with every exhale. He was always preoccupied with the little ones, reading stories and bringing colours and sketchbooks.

Another heavy night passed. He woke up, groping for himself, touching all his organs. He was still alive. Or maybe visible. He then heard a loud voice outside.

'We have no relatives in the South. Where do we go?' his mother whined.

'What happened?' he asked.

'Listen.'

The occupying army struck the already-broken internal front, playing on their fear and longing for safety. And they took over the local radio stations in Gaza, broadcasting bizarre orders and forcing the Gazans to some so-called 'safe zone' south of the Gaza Strip Valley.

He looked out onto his neighbourhood to find people in a circle of where-to-go discussion and confusion.

He muttered, 'If I didn't know the date, I would say it was the Nakba with all its details. But how can a killer define "safe zones"?'

Their home is near Salah al-Din Street—a street that connects the north of the Strip to the south. The displaced headed to nowhere—an endless abyss. The high numbers of displaced people fuelled their growing sense of danger, so anxiety and tension heightened.

'Stay? No. Where to? What matters is not to lose anyone.'

'We won't come back if we leave now. They will force us to Sinai.'

'What matters is not to grieve anyone. Just a couple of days, and we'll be back.'

All these conversations played out in the living room. Mothers were weeping. Children, too. All swam in a sea of perplexity. But he was the most bewildered of them all, tormented by the vexed question of the Nakba and displacement, consumed by the Palestinian narrative that repeated itself after more than twenty-five years of the Nakba. The same enemy. The same displacement. Even his mother's 'just a couple of days, and we will be back' reminded him of his ancestors' dreams that never came true. His mother was trying to convince his father, though.

'Nothing happens by chance,' his mother commented. When a family friend called, inviting them to stop by her home in al-Nuseirat, they had no choice but to say yes. They had a destination there, a destination in an abyss with no end.

'Pack your bags,' his father ordered.

He muttered again about how lonely the Palestinian were against the notion of home, trying to summarize it into a bag. We were so naive that we felt the warmth and familiarity of even numbers. We didn't deserve all this loneliness. What will I put in my bag? What memories will I carry? We don't have time to pack our laughs and scents; the sun is about to set, and the night unveils its fire.

He swiftly pulled out two bags: one for some clothes and the other for some books and mementos. In every displacement, we carry the most important things. Or so we think. But we forget our souls at home.

He packed them and stole a private moment with the house to say goodbye. He murmured: 'Our houses were small homelands where we took our first steps and spelled out the lands' lexis, all of which were homes containing our fragility, cries, secrets, and dreams.' He stepped to his room, lay on his bed for the last time, and sank into his pillow. He asked himself, 'I can only fall asleep on my bed. How will I sleep on another?'

The entire family prepared for the abyss. His father tried to contact any car driver, but in vain. The number of displaced Palestinians was so huge that they couldn't find a single car to take them. Shortly after, they found one of the municipality's cars, driven by a relative. And so, they managed to secure half of the family. The sun was about to set, and the other half hadn't found a car yet. They lost hope. But a family friend showed up in an ambulance and offered them a ride. The ambulance was too small to carry the eight of them, plus four individuals from another family. The whole situation was like being stacked in a sardine can.

He didn't say a single word, striving to figure out what was going on. How did he leave the house so easily? How did he say goodbye to his fresh dreams? 'If I had known that yesterday would be the last time I slept on my bed, I wouldn't have gone to sleep. Instead, I would have stayed up late, reflecting on my memories and the details of my home. If I had learnt that waking up meant facing the madness of war, I might not have gotten out of bed at all. But I was just preparing for a key class at eight o'clock,' he said.

On Salah al-Din Road, he observed the displaced Palestinians and the severe destruction the occupying forces left behind. By chance, they heard that the Occupation had targeted the vehicles of the displaced on Salah al-Din Road. They found it hard to believe. Perhaps they wanted to hold onto the comforting lie of 'safety'.

When you doze off in a vehicle, resting your head against the window, the breeze gently caresses you. You feel yourself melting into the captivating scene as you glide past streets—trees, and colourful buildings. Still, from the window of an ambulance, he saw torn bodies in flames inside bombed cars, as though their dreams were something that could burn. They chased survival, haunted by the illusion of safety fabricated by the occupation.

As his mother often said, 'Nothing happens by chance.' It wasn't a matter of chance to relocate to a 'safe zone'—as defined by an Occupation toasting their blood for 75 years—while being in an ambulance, witnessing shredded bodies burning on Salah al-Din Road.

He survived death three times. Twice while he was in the souq. The occupying forces bombarded a bakery there. He could hear the workers screaming, 'Oh, Allah, have mercy on us! Help! Help!' Their voices gradually faded away, and no one was able to reach out to save them.

Then, they made their way home before the Occupation fractured the northern part of the Strip from the south. And he, in the aftermath, lived on.

Haidar al-Ghazali is a 20-year-old from Gaza, trapped there during the war. As a child, his mother took him to poetry workshops and theaters. He writes poetry, but beyond that, he is a leader within his community, especially for the children around him. He had been studying English literature and translation at the Islamic University of Gaza for a year before it was destroyed in Israeli airstrikes. During the war, he organized events like 'Palestine Called Life,' a series of psychological first-aid activities designed to help children use culture and education as tools to express and write their stories, hoping to aid their emotional recovery.

The day he lost his cousin, he wore a pink shirt and returned to work with the children of the programme, focusing on imparting goodness and finding strength through that. In his own words: *Writing is the only thing that erases my pain. I write because what we are going through is bigger than all of us.*

A Jumble

by Fatima Hassouna

Translated by Alaa Alqaisi

I can feel how full my heart is—dense with all the subjugation that heaven and earth can embed on a human being. It's as if someone had opened the door and shoved a glowing coal just inside the threshold, and then fled, leaving my heart choking, or dissolving into the blackness around it.

What I want to know now is this: why have I been able to flee everything but not this subjugation? Why have I allowed it to pursue me, like a pack of rats? To hobble me at every moment; to bind me so tightly that no air can get in that would allow me to breathe in other feelings, perhaps ones that are new and different?

Yes, the word that besieges me now is Why?

I pose this question to myself, more than I ever have before, a question about all that has happened and all that might still happen. Why hammers at me from every direction. Why did I let them go without saying goodbye? Why didn't I give my grandmother that one hug, a final embrace? Why didn't I get the meaning of the code embedded in her narratives—what she told me every time she saw me? Why did I allow the passage of time, and my solitude, to steal all of these hours from me?

Why did I abandon myself to the four walls that swallowed me, without any reprieve, so that I didn't give the world a single chance to see me in my new skin, or allow the world to judge how far I'd come, or what or who I hoped to be? Why did I give myself up to war and death for so long, confronting them boldly and fearlessly, chest unsheathed, calling on death to come forward with its troops intact? Why did I permit the noose of silence to wrap itself around my neck so tightly that it throttled me—and yet, I hadn't even tried to say a single word.

I hadn't cried. And I had no sense of myself plummeting into the crushing depths, detaching from the I that is me. No feeling, not even once.

My *I* envelops me—it besieges me now. All of the possibilities I have held in myself besiege me: my past, my present, this war. They rip me to shreds, like any corpse torn to bits by splinters and projectiles.

But now, here's the difference: all those who have been ripped to shreds have died. I am still being shredded, yet I remain alive. I am still waiting for a why that gives me the definitive answer, that ends everything.

A why that puts the final dot on it all.

February 8, 2024

Fatima Hassouna is a photographer from Gaza and a graduate in multimedia from the University College of Applied Sciences. She has been documenting the war in Gaza with both her camera and words, capturing the broken childhoods of children, the helplessness of healthcare workers, and the surrounding despair. Amidst this, she also finds glimpses of people trying to live through the chaos—capturing quiet marriages or long-awaited reunions. Her writings reflect her personal experiences and observations of the war in Gaza. In July, she and her family were forced to evacuate their home in Gaza City due to orders from Israeli authorities, seeking a 'safe zone' in Western Gaza.

Day by Day in War
by Nasser Rabah
Translated by Hazem Jamjoum

Here you are,

preaching a silent sermon to a stack of the dead,

as if you are tossing a question to a vegetable seller,

then passing on.

Like this, Saturday continues its weary sprint to Thursday.

He tries uselessly to believe the newscast,

wishing he could flee from his own clothes, like his demolished house.

He turns in place from noon till night, like the hands of a clock,

wishing everything would stop—

Just until tomorrow, don't take me, O War,

what will I do on the morning of a day that's coming without friends?

Except that he sees no sign of the war's end,

nothing but the faint possibility that the last

tank will rust,

or the last soldier will die.

March 7, 2024

Nasser Rabah was born in Gaza in 1963 and continues to live there. He got his BA in Agricultural Science in 1985, before going on to work as Director of the Communication Department in the Agriculture Ministry. He is a member of the Palestinian Writers and Authors Union and has published five collections of poetry, *Running After Dead Gazelles* (2003); *One of Nobody* (2010); *Passersby with Invisible Clothes* (2013); *Water Thirsty for Water* (2016); *Eulogy for the Robin* (2020); and a novel, *Since Approximately an Hour* (2018). Some of his poems have been translated into English and French. He is one of the writers who has taken up the mantle of documenting the war through literature for posterity, as well guiding younger artists through this unprecedented crisis.

All These Words, but May I Speak?
by Basma al-Hor
Translated by the ArabLit Collective

We used to love walking through the streets of the city. Mayar would always stop us to take pictures or buy fresh mint leaves. I would point out buildings relating to an old craft, then we would talk about English literature. I would ask her whether she wanted to study the language during the summer break, away from academia that constricts our time and piles up. She said that happened sometimes, but that summers were more devoted to Ghassan Kanafani and Mahmoud Darwish.

I cannot help but think how much language is an ocean! I want to enjoy English, French, and my first love, Arabic. I used to race against time continuously, realizing that it was inevitable that we all gain knowledge of what came before and what would follow in life, and to walk with it at its own pace and in the way it desires. 'Slow down, anchor yourself. The one who is of two minds is a liar. You won't survive all this haste,' said my therapist, as the only thing I did back then was run.

In my heart, I deny the demands of deliberately clinging to the straw of the drowning one. I run to the exit from this cage of the siege, towards a mind that rejoices in the vastness of the Earth. I hope that knowledge will take me beyond those barbed wires thrown carelessly in the streets, which determine my fate and define which land I will stand on.

Today, a fear was ignited in me, the fear of being forced to cross it, fleeing the fires of hunger and displacement. I read about the policies of the Knesset and the 'State' in displacing us, and I am terrified.

Stolen livelihoods, deprived of free education, besieged schools. I think about myself, me with my reckless desire for knowledge. Me, constantly looking at the path of education, in its past, present, and future. Me, who couldn't fall asleep till 4.30 a.m. after the brother of one of my first pupils had said to me: 'This class was excellent, she loved you! Let us arrange more classes!' I kept twisting and turning—my mother woke up because of my constant movement. I was happy, smiling surreptitiously; I could not contain my excitement, I could not hide it at all.

What am I supposed to do now that the Occupation cuts me off from the one thing that defines me?

I was in my fourth year, about to graduate, and I aspired to work in Kuwaiti or Qatari schools. I was looking into the possibility of this, asking if they take on teachers from here, and if not, how could we make it happen?

I remember that, as I was researching for a debate titled 'Is it ethical to use technology in genome modification?' I read through the counterargument that genome modification is an attack on a person's right to identity. When did identity stop being a right?!

I am used to hearing this in the context of the homeland, the community, and young people's talk when they first embark on becoming independent beings. But is it the right of an individual? Every individual?

I had heard this in discussions in cultural salons and recognized its importance, I just never thought that one day it would come true… I took a minute to question who I was, yet again, as if I had never asked myself this question before. Throughout the entirety of the war, I kept asking myself: who am I without my quest for knowledge? Who am I if all of my books, diaries, and memories are destroyed? The 'State' severs the answer to this very personal question, so that fighting it is a personal matter from the very start.

In my final year, I started to step more carefully after running for so long, afraid that I was going to miss something, not realizing that I missed everything.

Now, after more than a hundred days of crime, I excel at distracting myself from this never-ending nightmare with other friendly nightmares that come to me in my sleep. I don't race against time anymore to find out what I have not yet learnt—grief and waiting have become my profession.

March 1, 2024

If I Start, I Won't Stop

by Sara al-Assar

Translated by the ArabLit Collective

Do I want to lose my sight? I don't want to see women, men, and children in the ruined streets, with nothing to shelter them, their eyes empty and lifeless as they try to escape death, to forget what has happened, to deny what has happened.

Do I want to lose my hearing? I don't want to hear the sound of the occupiers bombing people's homes. I feel the bombs shattering my own heart, not the homes. It is destroying me, bit by bit, I'm losing faith that humans have value and that there *is* a future. Do I want to have a future to live in? Or will I be gone before it begins?

I'm tired. Every night, I can't close my eyes because I think of what the future might bring. Every day, my exhaustion grows, along with my longing for the kind of days I once had in the past.

Writing is my only means of escape. I wonder what I want to escape from.

Death?

Or do I want to escape from the sight of what's going on outside?

I'm a teenage girl. But here I am now, my friends and I, looking up at the sky—not to gaze at it, but to guess which planes are closest.

We wonder if they'll bomb us, if they can see us, if they can sense us, feel our pain, or if we're prey in their hunt, one after another?

Day after day, we're dying. Our souls have become lifeless. We try to move past what's happening, but nothing helps in this state of humiliation, of injustice, of famine, of so many things. We're bored. And I want to smell something fresh: the scent of spring, not the scent of ash, and gunpowder, and blood, and death.

I don't want to hear people crying for their loved ones who are gone and won't return. I don't want to hear the wounded crying about the pains that won't heal, neither in their hearts nor in their bodies. I don't want to hear the sentence, 'Your loved one's home is gone, along with everyone in it.' I know I wouldn't see them unless I went to them, and I know that then, all I'd want is to go with them.

I want to complain about the injustice. I want to weep to my Lord and tell Him everything. But each word I want to push out of my mouth won't come. My mind has become empty: there's nothing to explain, there's nothing to describe, my hands fail me. Only my eyes scream for help. My eyes want to cry, but I don't respond.

I want to hug my mother, my father, my sister and brothers, all day and all night. I don't want them to leave my arms. I want to hear their hearts beating, but that's not enough. I want to wrap them in my heart and soul. I want to tell them things my tongue can't bear. I want to tell my mother how much her laughter makes my eyes seek her out, and how hugging her close warms me up. I want to tell my father that he has to keep on talking every day without stopping. I want to hear his voice all day. I don't ever want to lose it.

I want to tell my only sister that I don't want to stop staring at her eyes, her mouth, her hair. I don't want to imagine a day without her. And all I want to tell my two older brothers, who I don't see very often, is that I miss them, and that no one's on my mind but them. I want to tell them: 'Don't be afraid if we meet our deaths, but don't forget us. I don't want you to cry, because my heart has no wish to see you sad. I want you both to have a life where you can do whatever you want.'

I don't want to talk about my family. If I start, I won't stop. I don't want to talk about losing my family. I don't want my words to be.

February, 2024

Seedlings of the Dead
by Nasser Rabah
Translated by Hazem Jamjoum

Worried, I monitor the time on my phone. The event's coordinator calls to check up on me:

– Where are you now?

I'm close. Just a few minutes and I'll be there with you.

– You have the seedlings?

Yes.

– Good. Keep an eye on them, and hurry, we're waiting for you, and the kids are getting restless.

Fine. Ok.

A few minutes and it will be noon, the day evenly split, and the beginning of the event. I pick up my pace and canter towards the area with the tents of the displaced, where I will coordinate with the childhood follow-up agency to distribute basil seedlings to the children in the displacement camp. My role will mostly be to sing with the children and entertain them, while giving some explanation of how to grow and care for plants. It was hard to hear the coordinator clearly; his voice had to reach me over the squawks of the street sellers wedged up against one another on either side of the road, the cussing of bored passers-by, the horns of lethargic cars, the clacketing *carro* carts, and a stuck ambulance, moribundly trying to inch its way out of the Aqsa Hospital driveway.

I have to find a swift path through all of this to get where I'm rushing with a hundred of these seedlings in a plastic bag. I try not to disturb the delicate perennials in the ruckus of that high-strung hour. I dribble through the pedestrian corps, deftly passing some, jostling hips and shoulders with others, until I bump up behind a donkey-dragged cart, its driver maintaining a considered, careful pace. I try to pass him on the right, but there's a young woman whispering from under her niqab into the cell phone she carries in one hand, her other clutching the cart. I try the other way, but there's a young man in his twenties—head bent, grubby attire, his every step dragging as if he hadn't slept in days—also leaning against the cart's wooden platform. The cart blocks my path. I clock its cargo and fully power off my phone and recite the Fatiha under my breath. A person lies there dead—*mayyit*[5]—*kaffan*[6]—shrouded in the middle of the cart.

At that moment, I feel my soul rise up, my throat dries out, and my legs betray me, so that I have to lean against the cart. A mayyit with no cover but a kaffan for some dignified decency! A mayyit, and no proper car for a hearse! A mayyit with none but two mourners for a funeral procession! And a market's work-day bustle and ruckus all around!

– Events be damned. God, shield us from Your anger and disdain… You poor, tragic soul, what happened to you? Where is your family, you lost child? Where are your neighbours, you shit!?

The cart crawls towards the old cemetery. I follow in surrender, lobbing seedlings one by one on the kaffan, as sad as if we were old friends.

– If only your funeral were just a bit better.

A funeral as small as can be, just the phone girl, and the boy who's maybe her brother, and between them the body like a child in a cradle, rocked by the trembling hand of the dirt road.

---

[5] al-Mayyit is the term to refer to the deceased in Islam.
[6] A cloth in which a dead person is wrapped for burial; shroud.

The mayyit seems as though he has a plump body. It isn't bloating and there's no odour, so he must be recently deceased, not left under the dirt. Nothing about the kaffan's contours suggest obesity; the shoulders are relatively wide, and the legs are unexpectedly long—was he a runner? A moderate midsection, no sagging, no protrusions in the chest area suggesting breasts, so it's certainly a man—in his forties, maybe. The head is a little big, the hands not clasped at the belly like they normally would be, perhaps because he was washed and prepared in the haste of a crowded hospital. But those arms are long, very long—he's a basketball player. His limbs are all in place; he wasn't the victim of a shelling or a razing, he died whole and intact. A clean bill of health. Was it a bullet, or maybe shrapnel? I almost asked him his name, his cause of death…my thoughts hover around the poor miserable mayyit with no mourners, the children bereft of their basil—they won't sing or dance—the anger of the event coordinator, who is now cursing me I imagine, the displaced cast down that I've not turned up, the seedlings that I've scattered to keep this fellow company in his diasporic solitude, this long war and its end… I think of all this as I lean against the wagon, as if I'm the mayyit, not him.

I bark at one of the seated vendors to uncross his legs: 'Can't you see this is a funeral?!'

He complies, reluctantly, adding: 'Elbagiyyeh-f'hayatkum, may your life be the remainder.'

The driver, who is seated confidently and whose face I'd yet to see, replies: 'Hayatak-elbagyeh, may your life remain,' and he urges the donkey onward with a gentle flap of the reins. He keeps the careful pace, but his agitation starts to show as he calls out to people in the way: 'Behind you…coming through from behind.'

The funeral still moves at a slow, sombre pace amidst the chaos of the street. My head roasts under the sting of the June sun, and bits of sweat steal past my armpits and soak my shirt.

The young woman shoots several worried glances my way, but she doesn't say anything—she ploughs back into the ongoing phone call. As for the sleepwalker, I'd gotten a reserved smile out of him at first. No shared looks or glances since. I didn't really want anything from them except to ask about him. I've respected their grief.

We make it through the thick throng in front of the hospital and turn left onto a paved and less-crowded road, so the donkey speeds up to a trot, and we trot, too. We arrive ten minutes later. Looking in at the cemetery, I witness the tombstones shoulder-to-shoulder, no trees here—they were uprooted in the war and used as firewood for cooking—and no people out in the extended open, except for the four or five who are standing at some distance, above what appears to be an open grave. They look in our direction. I finish throwing the last of my basil seedling confetti upon my mayyit. The driver turns, and I see his face, with a solemn frown, streaming sweat with no sign of sadness. Maybe it's more like the face of a young man painstakingly at work.

Not directing his words at anyone in particular, he says:

– Hayyakum Allah ya shabab, ma-tshufu shar. Yikhlif 'aleikum.

God's good wishes guys, may you see no evil, and I wish your descendants to carry on your legacy (bye everyone, thank you).

The young man responds, addressing me and the young woman:

– Yalla, ya'tiku-l'afyeh.

Yalla, may He give you vigour (well done), and he walks away.

The woman doesn't say anything at all, she turns her back to me and leaves.

The people that had been looking down at a grave move towards us. The driver delivers his next words as if to dismiss me:

– Hayyak Allah, mister.

- What?
- Do you want anything, mister?

I bellow, pleading:
- Who is this person? Where's his family? Where did the others who were with him go? And you! Who are *you*, anyway?

Perched on the carriage, the driver looks around, making sure no one else is listening. He leans down, putting his weight on his elbow to come closer to me, to whisper:
- This is a gun, run mister. Weapons…you understand? Better for you that you move along.

Nasser Rabah was born in Gaza in 1963 and continues to live there. He got his BA in Agricultural Science in 1985, before going on to work as Director of the Communication Department in the Agriculture Ministry. He is a member of the Palestinian Writers and Authors Union and has published five collections of poetry, *Running After Dead Gazelles* (2003); *One of Nobody* (2010); *Passersby with Invisible Clothes* (2013); *Water Thirsty for Water* (2016); *Eulogy for the Robin* (2020); and a novel, *Since Approximately an Hour* (2018). Some of his poems have been translated into English and French. He is one of the writers who has taken up the mantle of documenting the war through literature for posterity, as well guiding younger artists through this unprecedented crisis.

Unable to Convey the Sound of the Explosion

by Husam Marouf

Translated by Soha El-Sebaie

Every evening, she would come with her face pale, her features almost disappearing because of frowning, and throw her body on the sofa I was sitting on as if she was throwing a bag of wheat. After the sound of the collision passed, she would advance towards my left thigh, and lean her head on it without a word between us, as if telling me *I still love you, I still choose to rest in your embrace.* I could hear the sound of a devastated waterfall pouring from her head onto my thigh to the point that one time I felt the dampness on my skin.

The one with delicate, tender features, eyes the colour of green grapes, and a vibrant spirit that seeped into every cell of my skin. She dreamed of becoming an interior designer—a dream the city of Gaza could not accommodate. So, she sought an opportunity to travel to Europe to work there. But the war came, and her family's house was bombed over their heads. Her father, mother, and little brother, whom she adored, died. Perhaps, it's for his sake she was postponing the travel.

One day, while I was listening to her sadness and trying to comfort her, I felt that I had suddenly fallen asleep or went into a coma. A strange brightness swept through the room, a terrestrial light, and after that I felt nothing, not even her.

I woke up from the coma after three days. I was in a secluded room in the European Hospital in Khan Younis. My brother was sitting next to me. 'What happened?' I asked him.

He said, 'God's will, brother.' I repeated the question, then continued, 'Where is Ramin?' He was silent.

The war, for me, ended right then. I am now in good health, but I am still unable to find a language to convey the explosions that destroyed my home. The explosion that stole my beloved from me and threw me into the unknown with this life. Every evening I sit in a tent next to my demolished home, in the same position I sat with Ramin. My health is good, but I feel severe pain in my left thigh. The same place she used to sleep in.

Husam Maarof is a poet and editor who is actively involved in Gaza's literary scene. He is the co-founder of the youth assembly 'Utopia for Knowledge.' He was awarded the Mahmoud Darwish Museum Prize for prose poetry (2015) and the Badr Al-Turki Foundation for Cultural Development Prize (2015), for his poetry collection *The Scent of Glass to Death,* and released his debut novel *Izmeel Ram* in 2020, published by Al-Ra'at and Bridges of Culture Publishing House.

A Song for Gaza
by Anees Ghanima
Translated by Alaa Alqaisi

-1-

Leave just one flower upon my grave
but don't water it—
so it can quench its thirst on the tears
that cling to the inside of my eyelids, and
await the funeral processions of my friends.
Let the flower upon my grave
revel in its radiance—
let it be proof of their life.

2-

In the same place, on the same seat
with you, Panic.

-3-

Out of wood,
unsuitable for burial,
the dead have constructed my room;
I am forever trapped
by graves I fail to feed.

-4-

I sit on the beach in Rafah, wanting to write a song for Gaza. I'm not sure what there is to write about the sea; all I can see are warships stretching out across a sunset, and a narrowing sea. What if I write a song with these opening lyrics: *A lonely man wants to cross the ocean and reach his shattered home in Gaza, where warmth awaits?*

March 10, 2024

Anees Ghanima was born in Gaza City in 1992, and currently resides there, working in Arab internet content support. He is a young web programmer and also a poet, currently displaced from his home in Gaza. Before the war, he was busy with his growth-oriented businesses and writing poetry reflecting on growing up in one of the most overlooked regions of the world. He is a member of the youth assembly 'Utopia for Knowledge'. He has been published in the local and Arab literary and cultural magazines. His debut poetry collection *Funeral of a Juggler* won the 2017 Young Writer Award from the Abdul Mohsen Al-Qattan Foundation.

A Country Forgotten in Immigrant Bags
by Hashim Shalula
Translated by Enas El-Torky

My soft voice was buried,
my cynical mockery of the world,
my eloquence tired of burrowing into language,
every centimetre I tread over has become a grave.

*

Illuminate my heart at least once, O soldier,
just once,
so I could speak.

*

My silence was seasonal,
at the break of dawn for example,
or the merging of two sagas.
But a sea within me was saying:
futility is temporary,
the dust will infiltrate beyond the borders of the siege.

*

My Bedouin nature is elegant,
clothing the gushing blood with the tale of another Messiah,
undoing its loincloth as if preparing for the intimacy of the lost storyteller,
gulping down the night like ginger,
and celebrating orphanhood.

*

I have been forever wary of eternity,
fearful of a hand plunging into the urns of ashes,
but now I am outgoing,
and talkative.
This is how cannons open their hearts to a strange poet

*

I have many sorrows,
the deepest of which was forgetting my sandwich in the oven,
and having it burn.
I held a funeral that day,
as if countries were forgotten in immigrant bags.

*

A new loin,
a new dagger,
a new Brutus.
The stabbing is ancient,
what's ancient is the stabbing.
O world,
the stabbed have become three.

*

War is a glass half full.
The glass rests against a finger, confused.
The owner of the finger runs,
and the sun whispers to the sea.
Morning is defeated,
and my heart overflows with the essence of the water spilling from the glass.

*

Our relationship to survival is strange,
like that of the back of a knife and a bird's neck.
A blade is forged for us,
and after a lifetime of failure,
we touch the windows of exiled stations.

*

Before the dove conceives,
it discovers the mistake,
and lays no eggs.
It leaves a note saying:
every slain man has wings.

*

All nights are one night,
all days are one day,
and times as well.
But my name is a community,
divided by the grievances of the tents.

*

I shouldered my ink
to paint the tribulation and a long-overdue salvation.
But I realized that the ink had spilled over my body,
because of the road and shaky footsteps.
The whole experience became a nightmare,
for the would-be painter.

*

My brief history consisted of a dozen wars.
I wanted a single war to create a poem,
to summon the heat of the audience's applause,
their mournful expressions, rising from their chairs.
I later realized that it was a more complex issue,
that man is forged by many wars,
more massacres and gallows.

*

Pure blood this time,
not mixed with the gunpowder of missiles,
this is what falls from the minds of those who were not injured by
the raids,

as they realize with their gaze the aftermath of the explosions,
an inhabited space that has grown into heartbreak,
and heartbreak that has grown into an inhabited space.

*

All the martyred tales of war
are still awake on the Bed of Life,
continuing their slow procession towards eternity,
aside from those of us who are not dead,
we were doomed since the first door was opened by the brutal hand
of October.
Our bones became a morsel in the mouth of a history that was here.
Perhaps it was here,
and perhaps we were.

*

The debts of a delayed dawn are paid.
A child falls like a leaf from the fig of life,
and with him falls rain from the heart of a waterwheel.
This is the story of our slain autumn,
stretching from the Nile to the Euphrates.

*

We emerged from the Scream,
we lived within it for a thousand years,
and we didn't ask from which throat we spilled.
Suddenly, everything went silent,
and screamers no longer had a voice.
It is said in lore that an epic has melted our traces.

Hashim Shalula is a Palestinian poet and writer from Khan Younis. He has published three poetry collections: *Telegrams to a Broken Fax Machine* (Al-Kalima Press), *The Wolf Will Eat Those Who Pay Attention* (Rawashen Publishing, 2021), and *What If They Knew We Were Strangers* (Rawashen Publishing).

A New Lease on Life (A New Life Added Each Minute)

by Nahil Mohanna

Translated by Osama Hammad

On November 3rd, came the last call for the residents of Gaza City to leave their homes and head south. Those who had remained from our neighbours walked out towards Gaza Valley through the corridor that was no longer safe, under the threat of bombardment and strict instructions to take fewer loads and bags. Our house was crowded with the neighbours' luggage because it was hard to carry them all, which was a good thing at wartime because we needed them after they besieged us and announced the beginning of the ground incursion.

Staying at Nasr Neighbourhood

Displacement to the south continued for several days through additional winding roads. Everyone left but we stayed alone, along with only one family in the alley, or should I say the ghost city that was once called Nasr Street which used to be swarming with people until late hours of the night.

Danger is close… Fear has grown…

I didn't know before that my neighbours were my companions, and dying with the group is a mercy.

For reasons I couldn't fathom, they started bombing the shops, and my middle brother's shop was among them. They annihilated it. The shop contained many goods and an electricity generator, which fueled the fire for about two hours. The shop was close to the house where we stayed and we were able to see the black smoke rising, forming clouds that covered the sky. My brother had a thought to take us there days before because it had a safe basement.

I don't know if I should be happy because we had a new lease on life or sad to see all the hard work my brother had put in over the years evaporate in front of him, consumed by flames and intense smoke.

The next day, November 10, we decided to embark on our second displacement from Nasr Street because the tanks were nearing. We didn't have the luxury to feel depressed or sad because of what had happened to us or around us. At wartime, there is no time for crying. You have to think about the next moment quickly so you don't perish.

We left for our relative's house, which was in the middle of the Remal neighborhood. It was only 300 metres away from the house where we had been staying.

At night, we learnt a tank barked in front of the house we had left. They besieged the only family who had stayed behind and they were evacuated through the back side because of the Red Cross. Everyone was holding their breath. Breathing, coughing, sneezing or even farting by mistake could cost you your life at such times. If you had a kid crying, you were dead. It's war! We had a new lease on life, for the second time.

We were around 30 people split into two groups: women and children stayed in one apartment while men and youth occupied the events venue at the tower. We had solar panels, so it was easier to do home activities, charge our phones, watch our favorite movie or watch news on Al-Jazeera at the top of every hour; but our joy was cut short... A week later, tanks advanced and reached our street.

Tanks Say Hi!

I had heard the word 'tank' since I was a child, but I only saw it on TV, in world war or epic movies. But today, on November 20, I saw them through the window. They were coming closer and growing bigger, their malicious cannons were moving right and left, ready to fire at any moment. I was still watching that terrifying thing for the first time, and yelled for others to come and see. When they came, they opened the curtains, and at that moment the tank fired three shells towards the window. The first shell didn't explode, so we ran away faster than greased lightning. Second shell exploded and the shattered glass was scattered everywhere. The third was fired at the moment we hid in the inner room. I think we were lucky that the first shell didn't go off or else I don't know what would have happened to us.

The injuries were cases of temporary deafness and minor scratches at the forehead, but I got the lion's share of injuries. I broke two teeth, my upper lip was cut, and I had a deep cut at the side of my nose. I bled because of my injuries and everyone was screaming when they saw the blood covering my clothes. They thought I was dead; but luckily, I had a new lease on life.

The tank left the street after the three shots and so we went down and piled up in the events venue until the announcement of truce—which stated that tanks wouldn't withdraw—saved us. We left our relative's house back to Nasr Street where we were displaced for the first time in the old family house.

The Declaration of a Temporary Truce

Our family's house consists of two apartment buildings with a gap between them. Each building had four floors, and each one had six families living in them. Only two families besides ours stayed. The lucky ones travelled abroad with the help of their kin living in Europe and some were displaced to some relatives' or in-laws in the south.

The seven days of the truce ended. We used them to clean the two buildings from dust, rocks, debris, ground cement and splintered glass. We patched the two houses up and closed the windows with nylon. Winter has caught up with us.

Danger was rampant, airplane and artillery shelling didn't stop. We decided that all of us should take shelter inside one house, thinking it would be the safest place. When my pessimistic brother told us that we will bake the bread at home because bakeries were going to shut down, we made fun of him.

Now, it became a routine. We knead and then bake with logs which we also used to heat water for bathing. One bath per week, whoever dared to disobey the instructions was denied baths for an entire week as punishment.

Now, we're four families in one flat. Twenty people, my father and uncle, are the eldest among them, distributed between two bedrooms and one living room.

The tanks didn't move for three weeks, thus a list of prohibitions was imposed: no lights at night, no loud talk, no radio, no going out of the house after 5 p.m. Luckily we didn't have any children with us or else we would have been bombed on the first night.

The repeated question was: do the soldiers inside the tanks know that we're here, just as we know about them and are watching them?

Our first displacement was on October 10, 2023, when the bombardment intensified in our neighbourhood and it was very close. They bombed the Paltel company's building which provided the Internet for Gaza. The situation was far worse. That night we decided to sleep in the house's corridor because we thought it was the safest place. They threatened to bomb a residential tower that was only 200 metres away from our house. We ran out of comforting words. Anxiety was the master of the situation.

They bombed the al-Karama residential block, the air strike lasted two hours and a half with what's called a ring of fire. We had friends on that street. We called them and asked them to immediately come to our house. They told us that they couldn't come because they were under bombardment and they would be hit if they moved.

I tried to listen to their voices over the phone as much as I could, as if I was trying to soak as much as I could of it, simply because I may not hear it again.

At midnight we heard strange sounds coming from the street. It was totally dark in the beginning. I couldn't assess the situation. I looked through the window, and when I looked closely, my intuition was confirmed.

The neighbours were evacuating. They had received a call from the IDF warning the entire area to evacuate as fast as they could.

Oh God, I was getting ready to sleep and now I have to pack my stuff and leave?

Leave to where? I didn't know any place in the world that's safer than my home. Two minutes ago, I was telling everyone that I could sleep only on my bed.

I wish I had a bag large enough to fit the walls of my home so I could take them with me wherever I go. There was no time to think; only five minutes or I will put myself and family in danger and maybe death. It's not the time to think, it's for fear. The Red Cross secured our route; our bodies were shaking, we were afraid that they would bomb us on our way.

We were displaced to my brother's house on the block where the old family's home was, in downtown. Certainly, it was the safest place according to the laws of danger. The whole extended family was forced to move to the same house, too. The numbers grew bigger, and the rooms were few. It didn't matter. What mattered was to be safe…

We agreed to just spend the night. In the morning, we would return safely to our bases. My daughter told me how much she loved her room and was attached to her stuff when she found out that I only bought one pajama and a toothbrush for her. I reassured her it was just one night...

On the next day, around eight o'clock in the morning, we left my brother's house and went back to ours.

It's lovely to go back to our home, it's lovely to fix it again, how lovely is my room!

But...

At 3.30, they called most of the neighbours' phones again to evacuate officially and completely. I packed a few stuff just like the night before; it wasn't necessary to pack a lot of things because we would be back the next day, or this was what I thought.

We left at 6.00 p.m.

Again, we found all the relatives in the old house. The house where I grew up. They were evacuated from different places; a lot of conversations were started, a lot of political analysis was exchanged, some thought the war would last for weeks, others thought it would last for months.

Their gathering in the yard and their careful listening to the news, waiting for what was going to happen and the fear in their eyes reminded me of the gulf war when I was my daughter's age. Damn that memory that only stores wars. Is it destined for us to repeat this history? It's repeating with the same details even though many years and decades have passed.

The next morning we all woke up for Fajr prayer as usual when we heard a strange movement outside. It turned out that the opposite tower received a warning that they were going to hit it; it was only 20 metres away.

The building was crowded with children and elderly, some of them were in wheelchairs. Everyone told us we had to hurry to the nearest UNRWA school. We fled to the school because it was the safest place until that moment, before it became a target.

We Had a New Lease on Life for the Fourth Time

On December 4, at 7 o'clock in the morning, they bombed the building opposite to the floor where we were staying. The sound of the bombardment woke us up. Ashes and dust were flying everywhere, obscuring our vision. Everyone was running to check on their people. After ten minutes of screaming and wailing, we found out that we were still alive and no one was scratched; we had a new lease on life for the fourth time.

Fragments hit solar panels along with the water tanks on the roof. We were now without water or electricity and the house was partially destroyed. In order to avoid repeating the same mistake we moved to the lower level and stayed at the house belonging to my uncle who had emigrated; it had been abandoned for ten years.

We stayed there for three weeks until the tanks withdrew after destroying the block where they had been stationed completely.

Nahil Mohanna is a Palestinian writer from Gaza, author of the novel *No Men Allowed* (Arab Scientific Publishers, 2021), the short story collection *A Life in One Square Meter* (Ougarit Cultural Center), and six plays.

A Fancy Farewell

by Haider al-Ghazali
Translated by Ibrahim Fawzy

Every time I leave the house,
I bid him farewell
for I may not come back.

Dressed up fancy,
to go out and about,
you would find me looking elegant,
and ready to step out
if you saw me during the war.

I do not love you, Death
I love Life and everything blue,
but my fate is always
sealed by you.

I am sick, a sick person
who loves a city;
a city that can give me only
the chance to die
the way I want.

March 7, 2024

Haidar al-Ghazali is a 20-year-old from Gaza, trapped there during the war. As a child, his mother took him to poetry workshops and theaters. He writes poetry, but beyond that, he is a leader within his community, especially for the children around him. He had been studying English literature and translation at the Islamic University of Gaza for a year before it was destroyed in Israeli airstrikes.

During the war, he organized events like 'Palestine Called Life,' a series of psychological first-aid activities designed to help children use culture and education as tools to express and write their stories, hoping to aid their emotional recovery. The day he lost his cousin, he wore a pink shirt and returned to work with the children of the program, focusing on imparting goodness and finding strength through that. In his own words: *Writing is the only thing that erases my pain. I write because what we are going through is bigger than all of us.*

THE SEA,
SLOW AND TIRED,
CARRIES ME
TO THE HARBOUR OF THE SUN

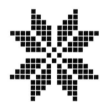

I No Longer Wish to Dream, nor Do I Long for the City

by Fatima Hassouna

Translated by Alaa Alqaisi

In the dream, I take off my shoes,

wringing my desires over the table of absence.

The absence grows heavier, thickening with each passing moment,

pressing down until it blinds me.

I become like oil floating on water—

a shimmering, murky green, a colour that feels like resignation.

The sea, slow and tired, carries me to the harbours of the sun,

where I sit with myself,

the heat of my disappointments,

and the fragile tent of people displaced and too poor to stand tall.

My mother yanks me back, gripping my ear with firm, unyielding hands.

'Didn't I tell you to stop wandering off every day?'

I twist and turn,

an egg sizzling in the big frying pan of this world,

peering into the vast emptiness that surrounds me.

No matter how loud her voice grows, it cannot reach me.

I steal glances at the fragile walls of this egg,

the strangeness pressing in from all sides.

Her hands pull me again,

tugging my stripped shirt off me,

peeling away, not just the fabric,

but something deeper—

the remnants of my history, my place in this world.

She lifts my face towards hers,

her eyes burning like molten shores.

She inspects me, her gaze relentless.

I study her back, silently asking, 'Do you see me? Do you still recognize me?'

I wonder, if far from this macabre reality, still exist—

honey-coloured shores,

with mint forests swaying in some distant breeze?

I stare at her, foolishly,

'Do caravans walking the smooth paths of lips

ever choose the rugged mountains and deep valleys instead?'

Her palm strikes the top of my head,

hauling me to the insignificant,

small things that make up our life together:

'Move! I need to start the washing machine,'

breaking the spiral of my dreams.

I follow her, trailing behind her laundry—

curling up tightly,

nestling among the shirts and trousers,

waiting.

As she bends to load the machine,

I feel myself curling inwards, smaller and smaller,

wanting to become a garment—a shirt, pair of trousers…

anything that could be cleaned and made whole again.

And a thought steals in: would she wash me too?

Could that big machine,

which no one but her can touch,

can it scrub off the stains of war,

the grime of exile,

and the despair clinging to my being?

I close my eyes tightly,

waiting for her hands to lift me,

to hand me over to the machine,

to let it strip away the weight of displacement.

Her footsteps grow louder,

closer, closer—

then began to fade,

further, further.

I open my eyes slowly,

as though fearing the darkness may never lift.

I find myself still curled,

still trapped in this fragile shell—

an egg frying in the vast, uncaring pan of the universe.

My mother's figure fades,

consumed by the emptiness that surrounds us.

Perhaps the machine has swallowed her whole.

Or perhaps it is the absence,

the endless void that stretches before us,

claiming everything in its path.

I try to breathe,

but as I inhale,

the light screams,

the sea roars,

and the world around me threatens to collapse.

I run—

above water, below water,

chasing shadows that twist and disappear.

A colossal hand flips me over,

tossing me left, then right,

spinning me endlessly in this vast, burning pan.

My mother is gone,

consumed by the absence,

and I cannot wake.

A sharp slap, a louder voice, and tears like broken glass.

'Wake up! We're on the brink of death!'

'What's happening?'

'We're being displaced. Again.'

'Where will we go?'

'I don't know.'

I stumble forward,

my eyes wide,

my chest heaving under the weight of the unspoken.

Then I stop, frozen,

tears spilling silently, endlessly.

The world, once so small in my hands,

has slipped through my fingers.

And in some dream,

I don't know which,

I lost the life I once knew.

Fatima Hassouna is a photographer from Gaza and a graduate in multimedia from the University College of Applied Sciences. She has been documenting the war in Gaza with both her camera and words, capturing the broken childhoods of children, the helplessness of healthcare workers, and the surrounding despair. Amidst this, she also finds glimpses of people trying to live amidst the chaos—capturing quiet marriages or long-awaited reunions. Her writings reflect her personal experiences and observations of the war in Gaza. In July, she and her family were forced to evacuate their home in Gaza City due to orders from Israeli authorities, seeking a 'safe zone' in Western Gaza.

Celestial Robots
by Nidal al-Faqaawi
Translated by Enas El-Torky

'We survive by the moment here, the time it takes you to like a post, the time it takes to switch off the alarm clock, the time it takes to call your son and he doesn't answer. Death is so much faster!'

—Hiba Abu Nada

A Palestinian writer killed in the Israeli bombing of Khan Younis on October, 20, 2023.

There's no time;

the celestial robots are in a foul mood,

and we terrestrials must find a way to communicate with metal.

It seems that signalling is of no use,

and carving four Latin letters in the yards calling for help

doesn't quite befit our souls.

Letters from Gaza

We have no time, my friends.

The flying insects must stop the game of setting fires,

while we decipher the explosive messages

and arrange the words.

And every poet should think about the final poem,

and cease using metaphors.

Ten metres according to the calculations of life,

so it goes.

Death, on the other hand, has only one calculation:

the distance is always zero.

The night, and the silence,

and the dim light on the walls,

are all misleading signals.

And you are as you are,

knowing nothing about the situation.

You look around,

shivering from the sensation of your shirt moving against your body.

You smell death up close,

but it's like fighting a ghost,

not knowing where it's lurking.

Nidal al-Faqaawi was born in 1985, in Khan Yunis, Gaza Strip. He holds a master's degree in psychology from Al-Azhar University in Gaza, and a bachelor's degree in psychology from Al-Aqsa University in Gaza. Al-Faqaawi works in the field of counseling and psychological support for children and youth. He has been writing poetry for many years, and his works have been published in local and Arab cultural and literary magazines. He published a collection of poems, titled *A Noon: Poems in the Cobbler's Cart*. He was displaced to Rafah. Israeli occupation snipers occupied his home, his library, and the 'poetry retreat', where he worked and wrote. They threw his books from the upper floor, burned the place, and withdrew. Despite such severe hardships he has persevered with his writing and documenting the experience of the Palestinians in Gaza.

Home Lost, and Nowhere Left to Belong
by Ruaa Hassouna
Translated by Nihal Shafik

We were used to waking up in the morning, while our mother prepared breakfast. She would send us off with prayers, each of us going our separate ways. Ubayda and Saja headed to school, while Mohamed, Islam, and I went to work. Sixteen years ago, she lost our father in an airstrike carried out by the occupying forces. From the time we were little, she poured love into us. To her, we were castles she had built, brick by brick, and carefully protected. She would never trade those old bricks for new ones by marrying again, despite her young age.

They had brought my father to her wrapped in a shroud, and she wasn't allowed to uncover him to see his face. The longing to see him haunted her. She said that he had said goodbye to her one night and never returned from work.

We were initially displaced from the northern Gaza Strip to my city in the South during the winter. We took everything needed to fend off the cold, from clothes and blankets to sleepwear.

My house often hosted strangers. They would sleep through the night and wake up in the morning searching for a tent. They'd knock on our door looking for a bathroom or sleep in a nearby field, enduring the cold and rain until the sun rose and brought warmth. In the mornings, we would thank God for the roof over our heads; and in the evenings, we would open our doors to guests. My house sheltered us all, including my uncle and his daughters, my cousins, my aunt, myself, and anyone who came seeking a place to stay. They found refuge from the night's cold or the midday heat of the tents.

That was until the occupying forces reached the city, and we had to gather what we needed to take.

- 'We don't need to take too many things; the operation in Rafah won't last long.'
- 'No, we should take the winter clothes too; winter might arrive while we're there.'

Where is 'there'? We didn't know where this 'there' we all spoke of was. We gathered our belongings in flour sacks, mattress covers, pillowcases, and bed sheets, just as it has been done throughout the Palestinian Exodus.

We knew only this place, my home. Five days were not enough to bid farewell to everything in the house and to tuck all the memories into a safe corner, away from the reach of airstrikes. I had to say goodbye to my bed, my room, my dressing table filled with all my lipsticks, the first dress I wore at a poetry evening—a black dress with light-toned flowers at the waist, needing only feminine heels to be complete—Bothayna Al-Essa's last book on the shelf, the glass grape clusters, all the antiques my mother collected piece by piece during every holiday occasion and visit to antique shops, along with the wool she used for knitting.

Even if they were hit, we would know how to recover them from the debris.

We kept delaying our departure, knowing the war wouldn't end, the negotiations would fail, and that we wouldn't survive even if we fled. We delayed leaving to make the most of the time we had, in a memory we would never regain, even if we returned one day.

When the shells came close to us, we began loading everything we had gathered into a large truck, crying as we did. As my mother touched the walls of the house, she filmed our small bathroom, the spacious kitchen with its red and black colours, the narrow living room, our bedrooms, the large wardrobe, the balcony overlooking the neighbourhood, and all our clothes that couldn't fit in the truck. She then turned off the camera and said, 'Take your last showers, because in the days ahead, we might not have the chance.' And then she cried. After that, we left for the place we called 'there'.

'There' was a small piece of land, cramped between a tent and an empty poultry farm. We set-up our tent, and as we unloaded everything from the truck onto the street, we sat on the sitting room furniture and cried. Then we began to set up what resembled a sitting room, laying the carpet on the tent floor and spreading blue sheets, so my mother could feel the warmth of their colour.

My five-year-old cat, Nono, was feeling anxious. We placed her in her carrier, where she panted from the heat. This was her first time leaving the house for anything other than a visit to the vet. There she was, leaving behind everything she had known for five years. Scared, she stuck her tongue out to breathe more easily in the stifling heat of the carrier, her thick fur only adding to her discomfort. When she stepped into the tent for the first time, she seemed astonished. What is this room where her entire family would now live, after having a house with five rooms? Where would she hide now? She hid behind the fridge, where spices and provisions were kept, and remained there for two days, refusing to eat or drink despite all our efforts to comfort her. She refused to trade our spacious house for a tent, leaving behind everything she had known for years. Yet, we insisted on making her adapt to our new reality, where we no longer had a home.

After two days, Nono began to move around in the tent. During the day, when the heat made the tent feel like a frying pan, she would step outside in search of a cooler spot. At night, the cold would drive us to rummage through our belongings for the heavy blankets we had brought.

After two months of trying to adapt, tanks suddenly entered the area, forcing us to pack our belongings and move to another place, and then another, and another...

Ruaa Hassouna is a Palestinian writer from Rafah who is actively involved in organizing events and initiatives focused on child protection.

Seagulls in Search of a Vanished Shore
by Muhammad Taysir
Translated by Alaa Alqaisi

Her small eyes held a tumultuous power, a loud insistence on delving deep into the labyrinth of disorientation, as she turned from the front cabin of the truck. Those eyes—the same ones that every Palestinian carries, no matter how old they grow—remain wide and steadfast, as if striving to speak some profound truth. Yet the maelstrom of exile and the relentless wave of catastrophes render their words cold, insufficient to convey the depth of what the memory of Gaza's people has witnessed, no matter how many metaphors are conjured to bear the weight of its story.

The man's hands stiffened as his gaze fell upon the three flowers pinned in the little girl's hair. He thought of how her mother must have chosen them in a distant, happier time—a time when mothers still had the luxury to decide how their daughters' hairpins should look. That was before the war, before motherhood transformed from choosing decorations to shielding their children's heads from the next bomb.

The little girl burrowed into her mother's arms, her blue dress nearly blossoming—if not for the thick smoke curling from the diesel engine of the livestock truck they rode in. The man, clutching the lid of a water barrel in the truck bed, watched this ordinary scene of motherhood unfold in extraordinary circumstances.

In moments like these, even a child's hairpin became a source of unease.

In that instant, the man wished he could confront any God—any deity—and ask: why, when mothers lose the scent of their scarves, when they are herded into livestock trucks, does God not stop the universe to correct such an error of fate?

This is Gaza: the land of unanswerable questions, disoriented seagulls, and startled gazelles fleeing from the vanishing silhouette of a city. A place where girls' dresses no longer bloom as they once did, where hairpins no longer sparkle in the sunlight. A land where mothers search for forgotten celebrations to pour the mystery of fragrance into their children's plates, above a city ablaze.

The man muttered Dante Alighieri's words to himself:

'There is no greater sorrow than to recall in misery the time when we were happy.'

His companion jabbed him lightly. 'You're rambling again, you strange man. It's the war! Of course, it does this and worse to men.' The man barely managed to tear his gaze away from the mother and child. He sensed the mother might be on the verge of tears and felt he ought to stop tormenting her with thoughts beyond her control.

The companion turned his curious gaze upon this peculiar figure, clinging to the rails of the truck's bed. 'You're from north Gaza, aren't you? Displaced, like the rest of us? We all have these moments—when we feel detached from the ground beneath us.' Without waiting for a response, he continued, 'Was Gaza ever this beautiful? Or are we just doing what everyone does when forced out of their homes—romanticizing them?'

The man replied wearily, 'You talk too much. Add that to your list of observations about what people do when displaced—they talk endlessly.' After a pause, he added, 'But it's not displacement that drives us mad. It's knowing the explosion was coming, seeing it so clearly, and doing nothing. What kind of madness rooted us in place as the flood bore down?'

The truck screeched to a halt, and the driver shouted from his cabin, 'Get off! I can't carry all this weight any further. Walk the rest of the way. Take your burdens and go.'

The passengers disembarked, including the talkative companion. The man wasn't bothered; in a land of endless wandering, distances meant nothing. Whether walked on foot or travelled in a livestock truck, the roads led nowhere.

As he walked, lost in thought, the man noticed the little girl waving at him—not with sadness or joy, but something unnameable—before the truck roared away, leaving him cloaked in its dust. He continued, consumed by his poor, pedantic companion's question: 'Was Gaza ever this beautiful?'

'Places like Gaza—forced into a relentless rendezvous with collapse and bloodshed—defy the simplistic binaries of beauty and ugliness. They cannot be called beautiful, even at the height of their brightest lights, nor ugly, even in their darkest hours. In such lands, where war has shaped existence before life itself could take root, the measures of morality and aesthetics shift profoundly. Stability and impermanence, calm and chaos—these become the alternate metrics of a grim yet enduring reality. These are the new standards of beauty for cities that have known destruction more intimately than they have known peace.'

He remembered seagulls he once saw flying near the shore as he sat by the sea with a friend. Bored by the trivial chatter of their companions at a café, they had wandered to the beach. His friend buried her fingers deep into the warm sand and said, 'Nothing about Gaza bothers me. Everything here is beautiful to those who call it home. But I can't shake the feeling that everything in Gaza is afraid, uncertain, as if a volcano simmers beneath us, and we've forgotten we need to act.'

A stray dog lying by the roadside lifted its head slightly as the man passed by, intoxicated by the weight of the sorrows pressing against his chest. Life along the long road leading to the displacement tents seemed to him like a grand defeat, the closing chapter of a life steeped in disappointment and surrender.

He looked at the dog's face—thin, emaciated, as if a single bark might drain the last remnants of life from its frail body. The thought lingered as he walked on: 'Did Gaza ever have any options other than explosion?' The question circled in his mind, unanswered, as he drifted into the cold breeze blowing from the west, growing sharper with every step towards the sea and the tented camp where he had found refuge.

'Perhaps,' he mused, 'if someone claimed Gaza had no choice but to explode, it would be an unjust verdict—one that absolves those who sparked the blood-soaked spectacle of their historical burden. As if they were saying: 'We have prepared Gaza for death. Let the ceremonies begin.' And so the myths were woven, the clichés repeated, and the absurdities magnified, without even a 'Godot' for the people to wait for.

The road was long. Before reaching the camp, he shook his head, trying to dislodge the sticky web of thoughts tangled in his mind. Rows of tents stretched endlessly in every direction, and the setting sun seemed to devour itself, ashamed of all those stories and the bewildered eyes trapped above the sands of the tents.

At the entrance to the world of tents, he stopped, confronted by the same scene that greeted him every time he left and returned. Each departure brought with it the same thought—a fragile hope that, upon his return, he would find the beach free of the piles of fabric, nylon, and misery. Yet, every time, the same ache pierced him anew when he saw the seagulls still waiting.

He sat down, laughing softly, then fell silent, his thoughts drifting:

Did that mother manage to collect the relief package she clutched so tightly in her hands during the journey on that livestock truck? Would there be something in that hurried humanitarian response to brighten the flowers in her daughter's hair? And was there, in this entire world, anything worth the cost of shattering the spirit of a child searching for a real shore amidst the stench of rotting sardine cans?

Muhammad Taysir is a Palestinian writer and cultural activist from Khan Younis. He has participated in numerous literary and cultural events in Gaza, with his work featured in several Arab magazines and newspapers.

Day 289 of the War
by Dunya al-Amal Ismail
Translated by Basma Nagy

I stand in front of a palm tree that is resting on the edge of space. I'm gazing at a place I never imagined I would live in, during my seventh displacement due to the war. I look around, observing the spheres of social life here—if it can truly be called life. This place is filled with fabrics of every colour and type, serving as substitutes for a home and a tent. I wonder how people managed to live through those miserable months of such an eyesore and devastation.

The sun's heat drains the joy of colour and life in a tent that has become a home and a sanctuary decided for us by rulers and leaders worldwide.

An absurd combination, which can come together only in Gaza, of words that evoke both pain and bitter humour that we know well, their letters are spread on tents and remnants of tents scattered in the vicinity and surroundings with excessive randomness: UNICEF, UNRWA, Qatar, the Emirates, Pakistan, Oman, and other countries of the world that have shown us their generosity and protected our flesh from the planes of the enemy who is no longer seen as an enemy worldwide.

Words that do not resemble homelands and should not have indicated them, I read them with sorrow; as they appear next to sewage pools, piles of garbage and children playing and frolicking as if the world is theirs—barefoot, disheveled, with dusty faces, their bodies darkened by the sun and lack of cleanliness covered by what looks like clothes. Some of them wear clothes of smaller size, some of larger and others are wearing only what covers the bottom of their bony bodies. Scenes that have become constants of the cursed war are difficult for the hearts that have been torn apart by the pain of the humiliation, insult, and oppression we have reached from near and far.

I am still standing in front of the lonely palm tree that has endured the fatigue of war and life, resting against the vastness of space. It is full of fruits, and I find myself reflecting on my life, my children, and our separation—how the war had shattered our simple dreams of reuniting after the two girls completed their studies in Egypt. I think about how I can find rest from the endless running and the constant search for work and writing. I almost managed to fulfil my obligation towards my family before the war disrupted everything.

It seems there is still much exhaustion ahead as I try to mend the destruction caused by the war in our home and neighbourhood. Despite all of this, I long for a normal, uneventful day—one in which I can sip my coffee slowly while listening to Fairuz, planning a future filled with the chaos of life and my persistent frustration with many details. How I used to dislike those details, yet now I find myself missing them.

Lost in my thoughts, I realize that war has robbed me of the ability to revere. Since when do wars heed the pleas of the heart and conscience? Life has been challenging for me in many ways, so what can I say about the hardships of war—and what a war it is!

I wake from my daydream to find my feet splashed with sewage water. A small stone was thrown by a child who was barefoot, with dusty hair and a smiling face. He believed the waterhole was the sea and then walked away.

Dunya al-Amal Ismail is a Palestinian writer and poet. She is also active in the fields of women's rights, human rights, and media, and serves as the director of the Creative Women's Association in the Gaza Strip. The poet and thinker Hussein Al-Barghouthi (1954-2002) described her as 'a special and unique Palestinian case in the sky of the image, leaning on the power of the moment.' Dunya was also active during the first Palestinian Intifada.

She completed her BA in Arabic Literature in Egypt and earned an MA in Political Science from Al-Azhar University in Gaza. She has worked as a journalist for *Al-Hayat al-Jadida* and *Al-Ayyam* newspapers. Dunya published her first book, I Saw in Gaza, and three poetry collections: *Each Separately* (1996), *The Ringing of Isolation* (1999), and *Not Him* (2010). She also won the Mediterranean Women's Forum Award in France for her story, 'My Mother and the Olive Tree', but was unable to accept the award due to the closure of the Rafah crossing amid the 2023-24 war in Gaza.

Now, Mohammed, Is Your Death Official?

by Hanna Ahmad
Translated by Soha El-Sebaie

Just now, I think that writing about you is a long eulogy... Is this a eulogy, Mohammed? Has the burden of our hopes in your return lightened on you? Has the word 'martyr' taken off your shoulders the weight of our daily demands for you to return? Is the word 'missing' so exhausting? O Mohammed! the man who kept running barefoot in the camp's alleys, trying to return home! Are you stopping your attempts now after nine months? Is your surrender final and overwhelming to the point that your return is no longer possible?

What is hope, Mohammed? What does this word mean? Does hope make sense in your case? And how would you have responded when we say that even after the state declared you a martyr, we feel you somewhere, still with us? And how would you have mocked knowing they issued your death certificate? You would laugh, your mouth would have been filled loudly with laughter and swearing, we would have watched your sweet laughter and said, 'Is it possible that this whole lively laughter comes from a martyr'?

Is Mohammed leaving with his entire being once and for all, just like that and so simply? We were looking into each other's eyes, into Baba's eyes, making sure that you will return. Even when I had some doubts, there was still some hope. I had so much hope that I searched for you as a prisoner in captivity, not as a missing person whom I don't know if he is still alive or just left. I searched, Mohammed, I searched for you alone and with the family. I searched for you among the names of those who returned from there, burdened, confused, hopeless, lacking vitality and desire to say a single word.

I searched for you in their faces and names. I showed them your picture, thrusting your face into their faces just like that, saying: 'Has any of you seen a boy named Mohammed?' They may not have heard your name, but maybe they have seen your face even once. I searched in every gathering for your eyes that shine like daylight, in all the names of Mohammed like your name, by the sea, between every tent and another, and in the hospital. My father and brothers searched for you among the bodies of the martyrs, among the unidentified. We stood at their heads, looking at their eyes, in which eyelids had blackened and life had been extinguished. Lifeless bodies that were only days ago, or even hours ago, perhaps, bursting into life, coming and going, eating and drinking, watching and getting angry and swearing, astonished and wondering about the meaning of all that had happened, objecting and refusing and screaming, and certainly wanting to return home.

How did those bodies, wholly filled with life, turn into completely still bodies, their mouths opening slightly as if they want to say something, as if the word 'goodbye' was still hanging in those mouths? We searched among the bones for your foot bone that we know so well. The failure to find you becomes a local anesthetic, an anesthesia injection, a temporary consolation that one day we will see you open the house door with your hand and say hello in your usual cheerful way.

Where are your green eyes? Where are your scathing comments about everything related to this country? Where are your fast feet that kept making their way to survival until the last moment? Did you feel after your running, which we do not know for how long, that your feet would separate from your body? Do you remember how you used to chase after the ball, scoring goals that were difficult for a goalkeeper to stop? Do you remember your easy start at the beginning of every football match? Did your feet fail you this time, so they were able to catch you?

Mohammed Osama Salman Ahmed, I hold his ID card and his eyes look directly at me, I studied his features as if I see him for the first time at that moment. 'What do you want to tell us, Mohammed?' I turned my face away from him. I tried to escape the burden of that look. I continued his story in my head, reciting his pain to myself and arranging its few events. I remember the details, repeating what happened so that no detail is missed, no matter how simple it seems. My hands are shaking and my throat is dry. My feet are angry and heavy. It hurts me that the sound of the phone is ringing on the other side while no one answers. I insisted, I called again, a fifth time, until I finally heard the Red Cross employee's voice. By then I felt weak, as if I was swimming against the current, and all the anger inside me turned me into a fragile body that doesn't know how to say a single word.

Nevertheless, in an automatic way I didn't expect, I told her about you and about January 7 when you called us at 11 a.m., in a mumbling panting voice telling us that they broke into your house, that you managed to jump over the fence while they were shooting at you, and how you survived two bullets that could have penetrated your body, but they penetrated the wall instead.

The call was distorted and lasted two minutes. You were unable to form many sentences, but we understood everything that happened. Our father called your name repeatedly, his voice was as if his soul was sobbing. He said: 'Mohammed, Mohammed, listen to me, come to us. Mohammed.' You were saying: 'I want to try to get back home.' Baba insisted that you come to us. The call was cut off and Baba drowned in a deluge of tears, he was crying bitterly. He said with despair I felt deep inside: 'The boy is gone.' For a long time, this sentence kept repeating inside me without stopping, 'The boy is gone, the boy is gone.'

The Red Cross employee was listening to my story, I heard her hands tapping on the device in front of her recording every word I said. She sighs every now and then, praying and hoping for your safe return and asking many questions about you, about your appearance, your features and your distinguishing marks. I told her about you; about your thick hair that resembles the colour of wheat ears, your 35 years of age, your wide eyes, your forehead that is flat like a plain, the old wound on your nose, your running speed, and the extra bone in your left foot. I told her that you were wearing your black winter jacket and sneakers, that you had left your cigarette pack and your cup of coffee next to your bed. I ended the call between us, and the employee left with her prayers.

A silence filled with noise prevailed, and the words kept echoing endlessly.

Sometimes I wonder what your disappearance means to an employee burdened by stories of absence, martyrs, wounded, and missing persons in captivity and those still under the rubble. What does Mohammed's absence mean to the world? What does everyone else, other than us, know about the meaning of Mohammed's disappearance? And you, who we thought would live long, that you'll outlive us by a long time...

Over and over again, the scene where you survived two bullets came back to me. I saw it in my dreams and woke up terrified with my heart pounding. They were short, unclear scenes that came to me as soon as I closed my eyes to rest them. The scenes returned to my head. I saw you running, I saw you talking to us, hiding behind the olive trees in an orchard called Shirin. You sat there feeling that your strength fails you and pain prevails in your entire body, and your knees could barely carry you. I felt you trembling, I imagined you taking a break until a sudden hope of the need to return home surprised you, and then you disappear. The calls continue between me and the Red Cross:

Hello, today is the 102nd day since Mohammed's absence, is there any news?

Today is the 150th day since Mohammed's absence.

I count them on my fingers minute by minute.

Today is the 200th day since the boy's absence.

I keep counting the days. This absence hurts me like a sharp blade piercing my heart. Every time, the employee tells me that she has not found any information about you. I ask her to just reassure me, to turn this great lack of understanding into an answer about you, to say: 'Are you crazy? Why don't you lose hope and give up searching for him?' Or to tell me that you were martyred last January, or to talk to me with a little realism: 'If he was arrested, why haven't we found his name yet?'

Why doesn't anyone put the truth in front of me, no matter how crude and violent it is? Why doesn't Ziad shake me and tell me that there is a great possibility that you were martyred and swallowed by this land that you love? Sometimes I try to explain your absence somehow. I told Ziad. I narrated your story to him from the first minutes with restless eyes and a heart falling from me towards the ground. Sometimes I fall into a sea of despair and tell him that you left and we will never know your story. He tells me with great steadfastness and faith, that you will return… You must return. Otherwise where is the body? He tells me that this confusing story will end happily. I tell him nowadays that they wanted to give us your death certificate, and that Baba refused to receive it because there is something that resembles certainty inside him that you are still alive. I open my mouth to ask him the question that he does not know how to answer: 'Do you still believe that he is alive even after the state considered him a martyr?' This question remains hanging in the air.

I wept, Mohammed; we wept. I cried my eyes out and we cried our eyes out. I sobbed and we sobbed… We spent the whole night talking about you, laughing and crying at the same time… We take out your hidden pictures, count the things you missed, borrow your tongue to repeat the words you used to say in a distinctive way and swallow the long days of your absence day by day. We miss you; this feeling invades us and we are sad because we do not know how to get you back, we do not know how to tell you that we miss you. We complete the scenario of your story that remained incomplete, we try to guess where your body fell as a martyr, and where is this place on which earth embraces you? Which sky are you under? Which people are you sitting among now? What do you talk about? And what do martyrs do, Mohammed?

The next morning, the martyr's first day, I woke up with a cold heart.

All I know is that I cried nonstop the day before.

I grabbed my phone, a tremble creeped into my fingers as I searched for the Red Cross number in the call log.

This time the voice came in a hurry—

I am Hanaa, I want to ask about my brother Mohammed.

Missing, since last January…

Mohammed Osama Salman Ahmed…

Again…I repeat the story.

Hanna Ahmad is a Palestinian poet from Gaza. She has taken part in numerous literary events in Gaza, with her poetry published in Palestinian and Arab newspapers.

When a Missile Lands
by Yahya Ashour
Translated by the ArabLit Collective

When a missile lands

by my house

I hope

that in its haste

it can see

that I have long braced myself

in a grave

dug by fear

and not a bed.

When the missile lands

I say, finally, death has come

but death, to my luck

shuns the ones most ready to die.

Yahya Ashour is a Palestinian poet and author from Gaza. He has authored a children's book, winner of the 2022 ACBPF award, and a collection of poetry. His poems and award-winning stories have been anthologized and appeared in newspapers and magazines in Palestine and internationally, in Arabic and translation. He has taught creative writing and literacy skills to both children and adults at various community organizations in Gaza.

Counting Has Become a Luxury
by Wissam Aouwaida
Translated by Enas El-Torky

How do I banish the sound of explosions from my head?
The bodies, the blood, the stench of death everywhere?
How do I wipe all this devastation from my memory?
The planes have crushed our souls,
and the tanks' chains trampled our hearts.
There is no corner of the memory where this war didn't punch a hole.
Blood has flowed from the body,
from the wall,
and from our streets, where we planted a rose in every corner.
Blood has flowed from our memory,
and even from the sands of the sea.
What sin have we committed, O Lord?
What sin?
What curse?

*

I want nothing but for this holocaust to end.
I don't want to write,
I don't want to read,
I just want this nightmare to end.
Perhaps we'll find time to bury the deceased.

Then we'll create a huge house for mourning,
as large as the city
or the rubble of the city.
We'll gather our remaining loved ones,
gather our memories that have been ravaged by planes,
and weep.

*

We left behind the city of our souls, O wretched world,
under the impact of bombs,
and death.
Where do we go now?
The entire city has become a gaping pit,
black rubble,
with blood flowing from every corner,
giving off the smell of death.
Where do we go now?
O world that has been watching,
for fifty-four whole days,
this ongoing massacre,
where do we go now?
Where to?

*

Natural disasters are a great mercy
compared to what's happening;
no earthquake lasts sixty days,
and no storm continues destruction nonstop.
Awaiting death, facing life under siege, everything is impossible after all this.
This isn't resilience, nor is it anything else.
What's occurring in this city hasn't even been seen in horror movies.

*

It's close to nine o'clock in the evening:
you ask yourself, what's left?

And you answer, nothing.
My breath, and the remnants of a life I'm clinging to.
The plane is howling,
and I'm so far from home,
and the city is gone for good.
The plane is howling,
over scenes of people fleeing, followed by death,
and hunger,
and fear,
and bombs.
The night, this enormous ogre,
perches on the breath of two million hungry people
in the streets, schools, hospitals,
the debris of houses,
and every nook suitable for sleeping in this winter.
And winter is a nightmare looming close to all this devastation,
howling,
and the plane howls,
spewing hell,
and death,
and all kinds of bombs.
A holocaust;
repeated every day,
every day,
every day,
and counting has become a luxury.

*

Where do I go with all this rage deep inside me, O God?
Rage for the city that dwells in my soul,
rage for the remains of all those children,
rage for this torment.
I want to explode in the face of the world,
in the face of merciless monsters.
I want some justice, just a little justice, or less.
Damn the war,
and the gangs of hell that can't get enough of all this bloodshed.

And damn you, ugly world,
for seventy-five days of public death.
Non-Stop.

*

One day I'll write about home,
our house,
the streets,
and the secret gardens we had left after the siege.
About the sea,
and the city,
that city that we railed against so much,
and cursed so much,
and mourned so much.
On that day, I will write with more than just letters of tears.
But now, it's time for rage.
I'm in dire need of rage.

*

If only this war would end now, and come what may.
After counting has become a burden,
hell expands over everything,
and every detail is hellish.
Then you tell yourself:
it's enough that you're alive,
you're assured that they are alive,
thank God,
thank God.
And you go back to fighting this hell,
and no longer dodge the shells.
Death avoids you by chance every day,
and you go back to fighting the same hell,
every day,
every day.
You carry a bag on your shoulder,
a homeless person fighting hell every day to survive.

And you ask yourself,
when perchance you have a moment with yourself in the midst of
all the crowds:
what's left?
How have you survived until now?
What's left of 'you',
so far?
Then you light a cigarette.
A cigarette, you miserable wretches.
A whole cigarette,
under the morning sun
in Rafah.

*

Twenty days in a faraway city,
Cairo.
All these people,
the noise,
the cafes in Shubra.
So many faces,
and friends too.
I mean some of those
who were lucky enough to be almost alive,
carrying a thousand wounds in their hearts,
a thousand infernos of anxiety,
an overwhelming mountain of sorrow,
and the pain of a thousand wounds,
and a thousand bodies that have grown cold,
without being mourned properly.
And my son, whom I left there.
My son, O God, my son.
And my mother,
my mother who has been consumed
by anxiety, fear,
and days of displacement.
And my siblings who were separated by war.
And the family, the family, O God.

And my house,
our house that was warmer than the autumn days,
and Fayrouz's songs combined.
And Tel El-Hawa,
the neighbourhood that has known me for forty years.
And the city,
and my father's shop in its heart.
My memory, and all that I am,
and everything destroyed by the war.
The massacre,
the perfect crime,
the shame that the whole world will carry.
It's all here in my head right now,
and I'm far away,
very far away,
but my heart is there.

*

What's left of you,
after you accidentally survived all the missiles,
and all the types of death that pursued you to the last wall?
You were forced to leave everything behind:
the city of your soul;
the streets that gave birth to you, and were born to you.
The house your father left for you.
And all your dreams, or what's left of them.
And family:
brothers,
and sisters,
and your mother, the apple of your eye.
And your son,
your son, you miserable wretch.

Your son,
your son,
the son of your heart, and life itself…
O, the heartache,
all of it,
all of it.
What's left of you?*

Wissam Aouwaida is a Palestinian writer from Gaza and a member of the Palestinian Writers' Union. His essays and articles have been published in various Palestinian and Arab newspapers.

---

* 'Hello, I'm Muhammad Sami Qureiqa. People call me Muhammad Sami, Abu Sami, or Sami. I have a lot to say. I'm really filled with rage because of the situation I'm currently living in, and I have a lot of important points to talk about.

Since the beginning of this war, I've been trying to cover all the developments personally, in an attempt to share with the whole world a lot of these questions. I started with: What is a homeland? What is belonging? What is a home? What is a roof? What is a room? What is a family? What is a friend? What is safety? What is fear? What is war? What is bombing?'

Muhammad Sami Qureiqa was a Palestinian visual artist, and friend of the author Wissam Aouwaida. Qureiqa was killed in the Israeli bombing of the 'Baptist' hospital on October 17, 2023.

I Break the Day, Unbroken
by Anees Ghanima
Translated by Alaa Alqaisi

I pluck a thorn from rotting flesh,

and swallow carrion whole,

for I know—from the bitterness on my tongue—

I am not the lamb of this day.

This day, I bring it down, it won't bring me.

This stone—I shatter and clothe it, and climb with it,

staring back at the one who dares to stare.

I muster an eye of lead for him,

a throat of steel for him.

I till the grass itself, folding this day—this day,

when I shall not be the lamb of this master,

with his plow and hooves,

with his mules and hounds,

with his deceit and his flock.

The master gazes from the tent's peak,

drool pooling over the remnants of flesh.

He gathers an army, hastening the siege

of shivers in the bodies of newborns,

on sands that flee through a narrowing pass.

The master gathers his trumpet,

but once again he falls—

crushed by the fist of this world.

'*I am terror*,' says the master,

'*I am the will of God.*

I come as I come,

and I am the earth's resounding echo.'

I pluck a thorn from rotting flesh,

and swallow carrion whole,

for I know—from the bitterness on my tongue—

I am not the lamb of this day.

Today, I bandage the lungs,

and open a vein to breathe the grass of my home.

Perhaps the enemy will step back

before legs standing upon fire,

quenching the thirst of my day.

Today, I rise,

two voices as one, shouting:

for the wounds and the stones,

for the forsaken upon their path.

I am abandoned—

but not the carrion,

not discarded in the void like some forgotten thing.

Today, I cast across all distances,

a declaration before the mammoth:

this lineage chooses to live.

Once more:

let the crimson flood the body,

and let calamity fall silent,

forever.

Anees Ghanima was born in Gaza City in 1992, and currently resides there, working in Arab internet content support. He is a young web programmer and also a poet, currently displaced from his home in Gaza. Before the war, he was busy with his growth-oriented businesses and writing poetry reflecting on growing up in one of the most overlooked regions of the world. He is a member of the youth assembly 'Utopia for Knowledge'. He has been published in the local and Arab literary and cultural magazines. His debut poetry collection *Funeral of a Juggler* won the 2017 Young Writer Award from the Abdul Mohsen Al-Qattan Foundation.

Faltering Memory

by Muhammad Ghaneem

Translated by Enas El-Torky

'My memories don't feel as though they've been pulled up by the root. Even if they fade, something remains.'

—Yōko Ogawa

− Where are you?

Here, where the tanks have arrived, and people are fearful.

− When you were displaced, where did you go?

There, where the false security lies.

− What do you say about your motherland?

As Ghassan Kanafani said, 'The motherland means not to have all this happen.'

− Are you tired?

Extremely, I don't know when this will come to an end.

− Turn around and enter that door.

It was a white door, evoking a soft comfort and coolness. I proceeded, feeling enchanted, pushed the door open, and entered. A bright white light enveloped me, and I woke from my sleep.

That was the last night I spent at home.

It was the day when paper leaflets rained down upon us, ordering the evacuation of the area where I lived, because it is a dangerous combat zone. I remember very well how I woke up groggily that day to the sound of children shrieking as they chased after the flying leaflets. As for me, it was as if I woke up from a dream within a dream, eternal in feeling, vague in idea and content, and never ending, or at least that's how I felt.

Are we really going to leave? The few hours we spent gathering our belongings and arguing over the idea of leaving and departing, I was full of resentment for my ancestors leaving their land, and here I am more than seventy-five years later, struggling with the shadows of those who departed. I glance at my crippled grandfather who lost his memory long ago. I constantly sit before him, and ask him about the extent of their apathy. Whenever they described our villages, they appeared enchanted by the evenings there, the landscapes, and tranquility, and lamented the serenity of their souls that abandoned them when they departed.

I constantly asked him, not expecting an answer from a man with no memory: 'How old were you when you fled the country, grandpa?' With a fixed gaze, without effort or searching his absent memory, he answered: 'We were displaced in 1948, I was 13 years old at the time.' At that moment, I realized that memory can't disappear all at once, and that there are scars in our memory that will remain forever.

I feel now how tough the decision was and recognize some of the signs that answer many of my questions concerning displacement. There, in the corner of the room, is my little daughter, who is no more than three years old, chasing after a butterfly that entered stealthily. And now all I'm consumed with is her salvation and saving what can be saved.

I look at my grandfather to the right and my daughter to the left and pick up all these signs; they tried to save their children's future, and the irony is that we are now living a hell in that very future they tried to save.

I turned to my grandfather, and then to my daughter... Then I wept and screamed... My decision is to flee to a place of false security and not to remain within the scenario of the game of doubt, possibility, and conjecture. I decided to survive with my family, and nothing else.

Fear consumes our hearts, and the sounds of heartbeats become louder and louder until they drown out the sounds of the shelling that has recently begun to intensify.

We arrange our belongings in a large truck and leave for the unknown. We leave after reducing the house to a few items and colourful carpets. We depart from the groves of sentiment, the chambers of memories, and the walls of warmth and shelter, to a barren desert with no water, no hope, no safety, and no warmth.

We settle in Al-Mawasi, Khan Younis, very close to the sea. We pitch our tents, sleep in disappointment, and wrap ourselves in fear, to shield us from the cold. Sleep has forsaken our eyes, and tears pour down on our frustrations, soaking them until they sprout forests of ash. The longer the war drags on, the more it covers our bodies, and we become discoloured with its hue day after day. With each day passing there, the questions grow bigger and feed on the doubts and apprehensions within us. The questions have grown, until the question marks faded away.

We go around in circles, prayers, supplications; we have become dervishes:

> O God, why do we keep coming back to You every time?! Why do we plead with You to end our suffering, when we are the ones who created all these wars and images of destruction?! Why all this anticipation of Your loving hand to stroke our hearts, as if nothing has happened? You are the One who left our choices

> unlimited, and never intervened between cause and effect. My obsessions consume me, and questions suffocate my narrow throat. If we are part of You, and You want to bring us back to You, we are content, O God. Everything has become extremely crushing, and our hearts can no longer endure. O Allah, fill us with You so that we do not feel hollow and desolate…

I spin in a vast void and I feel nothing. I continue to spin between our tents and touch nothing, I spin and spin until I fall to the ground.

For thirty years I tread the ground with trembling footsteps, and this is the first time I feel the earth telling me: 'You are burdened, take it easy, and reduce your load.' I fainted, I fell to the ground, and came in the morning, as if nothing had happened.

Each time night falls, I attempt once again to reach for the sky with my hands, but my body is still heavy, drawing me to the ground as if I were shackled to stakes and tied to the ground from all my limbs, like a tent resisting all forces of nature that want to uproot it from its place but cannot. My soul is still trapped in my cumbersome body, and all the souls that have passed away are calling to me. This mud suffocates me, and my soul revolts under it.

When will the rain fall, dissipating this sand, so I can shed my heavy garment, and my soul can be quenched, shaking itself out of the mud and departing, embracing all the reasons for survival and shedding its tears so that the rain increases, before returning where it belongs. The higher it soars, the sand dissipates in the ground, and when it arrives, flowers and fields sprout.

The prophet of wisdom is lost in the wilderness of queries:

> When will the thirsty souls be quenched, O God? When will You fill them with Yourself, so that they do not need anyone but You? O God, I am weary, fill me with You,

and deliver me from the desert of the body to the fields of the soul.

Every day that passes in my tent, I'm haunted by obsessions of uncertainty and doubt, reeling between reality and illusion. The questions increase and grow every time I wake in the morning and see the roof of the tent. I gasp in fear and ask in desperation: where am I? Is this real? Will we stay like this forever?! I get lost on the path between reality and illusion. I travel it daily to find an answer, constantly staggering. I travel back and forth; often I don't know where to settle, so I continue to wander and hope for deliverance, sleeping in my displacement tent, awaking, sleeping, awaking... No change, no life, no salvation.

In a country teetering on the edge of everything, memory and oblivion, doubt and certainty, water and land, night and day, peace and war, home and tent, life and death, past and present, I've assumed the role of the country, and I am standing between everything; my doubt and my certainty, my misgivings and my reality, those who stayed and those who left.

I'm now standing on the edge of an old harbour that extends through the sea, raising my hands up high. The wind mixed with the spray of salty sea water fills my mouth, my shirt flutters behind me like the country's mournful flag. I stand in surrender to the wind; let it take me where it will, the reasons for staying and departing are one and the same.

In the midst of this desolation, my grandfather passed away silently. We woke up later to find that he had departed, clinging to the scars of his memory even in the final days of his life.

Muhammad Ghaneem is a Palestinian writer from Al-Maghazi refugee camp. He authored the short story collection *The Limbo*, which won first place in the 2020 Naji Naaman Literary Prize for Short Story (Palestinian Ministry of Culture – Ramallah).

Facebook Wall

by Amira Hamdan and Bahaa Shahera Rauf
Translated by Basma Nagy

- Amira -

I'm not sure how old I am now; I forgot, and that happened because I wanted to forget. I pick through some memories from the years, selecting a few, as many remind me of the depth of my loss. I walk through time with no real connection to it. I let it pass by, I numb it, I count it, I forget it, I carry it on my back. Eventually, I grow tired of it and throw it away, just to find some space to breathe. I stand before time like a moviegoer who will leave soon.

Since the day I was born, I've never felt attached to time. I let it cry and laugh behind me as it pleases, and whenever it waved its hand to call me, I walked by as if it didn't concern me at all. This indifference seemed to annoy time, prompting it to seek revenge. It raced ahead of me, making me feel as if I were carrying fifty million years on my shoulders.

With a malicious smile, time wouldn't allow me to think without its weight pressing down on me. I challenged it and, in a way, I defeated it. It screamed and complained, aggrieved. I told time that I wasn't to blame; it had wasted me, just as I had wasted it!

Soon, it will be gone forever, no matter what happens. In the morning, I will leave the tap water running after washing my face and step out into the world without a destination in mind. When a bus stops for me, I will get on without questioning where it leads. I'll hop on and off at unfamiliar stations—places that neither know me nor I know them. I will listen to the sound of the wind through the window and gaze into the emptiness until I can no longer see or hear anything around me.

When I tire of the endless journey, I will stretch out beneath any inviting tree and not worry about the time. I will let time take the lead and surrender to it. I want to wander through countless unfamiliar streets, passing through them like a scent that awakens memories long forgotten. Perhaps I will discover my soul and finally understand who I am...and maybe life will remember that I am its forgotten daughter!

Amira Hamdan is a Palestinian writer from Gaza and coordinator of the 'Baytakom Amer' initiative, which focuses on reviving Palestinian heritage.

- Bahaa -

After I broke up with my girlfriend, I felt very sad about what had happened between us. The sadness lingered, and I refused dating anyone else for a long time. Years later, a girl came into my life and changed everything, shaking up all my previous decisions.

Because of my deep fear of experiencing that heartbreak again, I kept my distance and remained reserved about the relationship until I eventually succumbed and started our journey as a couple. I was captivated by her, and my mind was enchanted by her beauty. We discussed the most unusual topics, and I often shared my peculiar desire to pour tea over rice and taste it. I painted vivid pictures in her mind of what that flavour might be like. In return, she expressed her strong desire to open my heart and *unblock* it, telling me that I was one of the strangest people anyone could ever meet.

As the years went by, I went through a severe bout of depression that detached me from all that was natural in the world. Her inherently positive nature made me distance myself from her. I didn't want to burden her with the darkness that filled my heart, especially since she embraced life so passionately. She often encouraged me to wear pink, saying it was a way to show the world that I loved life; and I refrained from it, reminding her that it was a colour for girls, but actually afraid of embracing that faint light within me.

After all these years, I still remembered her, but I didn't dare to message her, even though we were friends on social media. Her picture repeatedly tugged at my heart, insisting that our beautiful connection should be rekindled.

Today, I opened her profile page, only to find that all her friends were mourning her. I couldn't believe it at first until I came across her sister's obituary. She had been killed by the brutal war machine last December. I couldn't control my emotions and started crying, tears flowing for her just as they had when my beloved left me.

I felt immense guilt about all the time we had spent apart. She was so sweet and loved listening to the Egyptian band Cairokee. She was full of life, and it had been unbearable for me back then. Oh God, this sadness is overwhelming for any human being. Why her, in particular? I can't handle this harsh separation at all. She was too beautiful to die and too radiant to be laid to rest in a barren cemetery, surrounded by everything that contradicts life.

The last message she sent me was a distorted clip from her favourite band's song, saying, 'No matter how long your night is, get up and wear pink.'

I never expected that the songs between us would turn into a harsh memory, and I never imagined that a clip from a song would turn into a nightmare.

Her name was Lynn. In Arabic, Lynn means tenderness and softheartedness, and she was soft-hearted, by God, and I am at the peak of my sadness as I write about her in the past tense.

We will wear pink, sweetheart. No matter how long the war lasts, we will wear pink in the end.

Bahaa Shahera Rauf is a Palestinian writer residing in Deir Al Balah near the historical site of Al Khidr. Along with a group of friends, he actively participates in assisting various places in Gaza. Ever since the war, Bahaa has been struggling with depression, but that hasn't stopped him from assisting the community as he feels he has a national duty to fulfill and a national struggle to follow through for the people. He exemplifies the steadfast spirit of the people of Gaza, as despite the fears and anxiety they carry about what's to come, they also have an inherent pride in their resilience and the strength of their thoughts and concepts.

Eight Fingers

Written and translated by Basman Eldirawi

I count things,

as if I'm counting the hours until sunrise,

then I count the hours of the morning, hoping the sounds will end.

I count the sounds of the missiles, and how many times I could have died,

I count my loaves, reminding myself not to eat my brother's—

don't let him die hungry.

I count the clouds in the sky

before they're covered in dust from the missiles sent for death.

I walk on the street

counting what houses and traces remain;

I've walked here once, I've laughed here once, I've cried here once.

So I don't forget how the city looks,

I've memorized it before it's hung naked from some gallows.

I count the moles on my body,

as if to say goodbye, before the enemy cuts off a limb.

I count poems, thinking,

which of them will be killed, unfinished, like an unborn child;

some have not even taken a breath, like a baby born too soon.

I count my friends, before the breaking news;

yesterday they were ten, and I counted them on my fingers—

but today I woke up to eight fingers.

Basman Eldirawi is a 29-year-old physiotherapist and writer from Gaza. He graduated from Al-Azhar University in Gaza in 2010. He has a passion for movies, music, and working with people with special needs. Since the war began in 2023, he has been writing about the experiences of the Palestinian people in Gaza to shed light on their plight.

A Scarf

by Aseel Salama

Translated by Hadeer Mohamed

Mostafa is his name, and Aisha is his bride's name. The war bore witness to their wedding; it even shared their displacement tent, joining them for breakfast the morning after. 'Do not be afraid, Aisha,' he whispered to her as she clung to him, startled by a missile attack nearby. 'I'm frightened,' she replied, shivering. He embraced her, tenderly stroking her hair until the war receded to another city.

They had married in Rafah two weeks prior, in a hurried ceremony due to the ongoing war, before being displaced to Mawasi Khan Yunis. Mostafa chose to accompany his wife's family in their displacement, honouring her wishes. He pitched a tent for them near her family's, as her parents wished to keep a watchful eye on their beloved daughter.

Mostafa's own family had been displaced from Rafah two months earlier, settling in a tent south of Mawasi Khan Yunis. Unfortunately, they found themselves caught in the outbreak of war, moving from one danger to another. The conflict inflicted wounds on many, including children, women, and men. Mostafa felt profound sorrow as his father suffered a fatal injury from shrapnel to the head. They hurriedly buried him among the many casualties. His mother sustained a shrapnel injury to her spine, leaving her unable to stand or walk. Mostafa's brother, Ahed, took on the responsibility of caring for her, and she now resided with him and his wife in their tent. She couldn't attend her son Mostafa's wedding due to her injuries.

'It's the war; it truncates everything,' Mostafa consoled his mother over the phone while waiting in a long line for bread. 'I have a gift for you and your bride,' his mother announced. He expressed gratitude and promised to visit her, no matter the dangers of the road.

Returning to the tent with the bread, Mostafa ruminated on how war abbreviates lives and lengthens queues for essentials like bread, water, and medicine. Entering the tent, he felt butterflies in his stomach, missing his bride who couldn't bear an hour without him. She had just applied lipstick when he arrived, and she leaped into his arms, embracing him tightly. 'You were gone too long; I missed you,' she flirtatiously whispered in his ear. Stepping back, she was pulled into his arms again, his desire evident as he wordlessly savoured her presence, enveloped in profound silence save for the rustle of their clothes.

Mostafa shared his plans for the next day with his wife. Alarmed, she asked, 'Can I accompany you?'

'It would be my pleasure, but I fear for your safety. I'll return before you know it,' he reassured her.

The following morning, Mostafa set out to visit his mother, navigating streets worn out from a night of violence. Checking in on his mother, brother Ahed, and their families, he swiftly retraced his steps back to his wife, bearing two gifts. He took a carriage, its coachman kept on singing, and when he took a moment of silence, Mostafa asked him 'Do you love her?'

'Who is she?' the coachman responded.

'Your wife, the one you're singing about,' Mostafa said.

'Of course I do,' the coachman responded, 'but the war took her life along with our kids'; I'm all alone now.' The coachman lamented.

A moment of heavy silence passed. The coachman turned to Mostafa and asked: 'And what about you? Do you love her?'

'Of course I do; we are newlyweds, I'm crazy about her,' Mostafa said. 'I took a risk going down this long road for her sake. My mother gave me a watch belonging to my late grandfather as a present for me, and another gift for my wife,' he added a moment later.

'It's surely a hand-embroidered dress,' the coachman said.

'I won't tell you, I will keep it a secret till my bride takes it,' Mostafa responded.

As the carriage pressed on, a nearby sniper took aim at the coachman, firing shots in jest. Ignoring the danger, the coachman continued singing. Suddenly, a bullet grazed his head, and then another struck him fatally. Chaos ensued as the horse was hit, bringing the carriage to a halt. Mostafa leaped out, sprinting towards his tent where his beloved awaited. Unmindful of the danger, he pressed on, determined to deliver his mother's gift. Despite bullets flying perilously close, he persisted, until a shot to the leg forced him to crawl. Another bullet struck his arm, but still, he inched forward.

A final bullet found its mark, and Mostafa fell; a purple scarf near his heart, now soaked in his blood.

Aseel Salama is a 24-year-old woman who has been documenting people's lives under bombardment in the city of Rafah. Her family home has become a shelter for many displaced people, and Aseel chronicles her daily life in that home, which she shares with her five nieces and nephews. Aseel writes with the sincere hope that her words will move enough people to bring an end to this war. For her, writing serves as therapy, helping her and other Palestinians cope with what they are experiencing.

Springtime in the Cemetery
by Batool Abu Akleen
Translated by Ibrahim Fawzy

I want a grave with a marble headstone

that my loved ones will water,

where they will place flowers,

weeping when the longing lacerates their eyes.

Their tears won't reach me so I won't grieve.

I want a grave just for me for my friends to talk to me

where I'll have the right to be alone one last time.

I want a grave that doesn't touch another,

so my beloved can plant a bougainvillea to shade me from the summer sun,

to dress me in a purple gown in the spring,

to give me a warm cover in winter when its leaves fall.

I want a grave in a cemetery,

with neighbours who have wrapped themselves in life,

flirted with it,

planted a kiss on each of its cheeks, then slumbered.

I want a grave,

I don't want my corpse to rot in the open road.

February 26, 2024

Batool Abu Akleen is a poet and translator from Gaza, Palestine. She started writing at the age of ten, and at the age of fifteen, she won the Barjeel Poetry Prize for her poem 'It Wasn't Me Who Stole the Cloud,' which was published in the Beirut-based magazine *Rusted Radishes* and later included in the Italian anthology *Of Water and Time*. Akleen's poetry has been translated into several languages, including English and Italian, and featured in numerous international publications.

From 'Burrow'

by Rawan Hussein

Translated by Wiam El-Tamami

I hide in a burrow. I have salt and bread.
And because my time has not yet come, I sneak up to the windows,
like the drones do.

I watch the strikes of blues and reds:
lightning that thunders, bombs as they blast.
I see small children, wrapped in their shrouds.
My senses harden. Their shy tears fall; I cry on their behalf.

We conquer time, hostages, the wind, tears of women and the sky.
We stumble around in our shelters: where is the way out?
We are alone here, dancing under the rubble, peeling
the orange skins, crushing olives with rocks.
Wrapped in white, though we haven't lived for a day.

My mouth has been closed for days.
I leave the walls of my head, the agendas;
I can't see my face in the mirror—
Could it be, am I really gone?
This is how they hover around us: ghosts, mouths shut.
They don't see their battered faces; they watch
as space is extinguished, growing closer to a truth
beyond the reach of the living.
The bread and those crossing over, both consumed by time.

The moist earth holds the human remains.
In a wood stove that the wind has tired of lighting,
the mothers place whatever memories are left.
The houses step over us; the sidewalks gnaw on our bones;
the sun cowers before our wrinkled faces, grows cold.
Our strength falters and we rise, dying in two different dimensions,
and in a third, voices fall upon us and we wake like the sun, beaten.
Our eyes well up with tears
and we have no idea why.

Rawan Hussein is a young poet from Rafah. She is a beautiful woman with a lovely bob-cut hairstyle that makes the heart yearn for her freedom to sail in the open air. Soon after the war began, she shared in a statement that 'a cure for survival' in this time of war is the necessity of humankind 'to empty in any form, whether by dancing, singing, drawing, sculpture, shouting [...] but I write.' Her work brings to life the grief at the core of the conflict in Gaza.

Writing While Searching for Hope: A Year after the War of Annihilation
by Mahmoud Alshaer
Translated by Soha El-Sebaie

It has been more than a year now. I am still undergoing an intense war in the Gaza Strip. It is not easy for me to deal with the traumas I am exposed to, which push me to make decisions, most of which I regret now, as I write this letter. I wonder how the future of the war can be read, and how the plans being implemented against me can be read? But how can I try to look to the future when I cannot guarantee being alive in the next few minutes?

Anticipating the future and working on building paths that lead to it cause me pain, as if I am recognizing amputation. This war not only robbed me of the people who were killed, but it also robbed me of the possibility of meeting again with all those who travelled abroad to escape it. My entire family has travelled; my mother is accompanying my son Majd in Turkey to get medical treatment for both of them, and my brother and his family are in Egypt, in addition to all my uncles and their sons and grandchildren.

I lose all of them whenever I try to imagine the future, create paths and practice to build any action that saves me from the emptiness and the helplessness based on falling into this void.

Silence devours me, and memories of the past keep popping up in front of me. It hurts me to realize that everything I see when my eyes fall on a picture in my mobile phone has been completely destroyed. This realization hurts me, but I don't stop looking at what the war hasn't taken from me. Despite the cruelty of realizing what has already been taken away, I still believe that I can rise again if I survive this war and that all the losses haven't taken away my ability to practice the act of cultural production. I believe that nearly two decades of life under siege have trained me well in resilience. But I still want this war to stop.

It hurts me to anticipate the future, and to anticipate the practices, actions, and exercises that lead to cultural or artistic production. I wonder how we will overcome the lamentation and sadness over everything that the machine of war and destruction has erased.

How will I survive?

I Am Writing Now While Searching for Hope

I am writing now while searching for hope, and what I am searching for is not just a feeling, but a definition and understanding of the distance between gaining hope and losing it. I am living the 116th day of the war. I listened to a child from inside Gaza City appealing to be evacuated from a car being shot by a tank. Despite the fear, hope was high in the child's voice as she said: 'Uncle, we are trapped inside a car and the tank is next to us, shooting us.' Then I heard the child screaming after being hit by more than one fatal bullet.

I have reflected a lot on the last moments filled with hope for a chance to escape death. But time passed and the child became an additional number among the victims of the war of life annihilation in the Gaza Strip.

I am writing now in poor language, my words and personal dictionary are no longer suitable for the moment I am living, as all the vocabulary I think of to use in writing seems to have a meaning that is not enough to explain what we are suffering in the war, vocabulary that cannot explain what has changed in my lifestyle and principles. I am afraid to say 'I looked at the sky' because every look is to follow the sound of a warplane that wants to bomb us.

I avoid using the word 'good morning' or 'good evening' because goodness cannot come in the context of war. And so, I go on as a poet whose language was destroyed by war and left him in emptiness; busy searching for security and uncertain hope.

I write now with a memory without witnesses, as if I am pointing to the void whenever I remember my friends, my happy moments, my favourite places, the sidewalks of the streets and the landmarks of the place. My personal oral history is my only witness to my identity and who I am.

The frightened person who writes to you is neither a hero nor a legend. I am a writer from Gaza who has a few simple dreams, the most important of which is to be able to get enough food and water.

The frightened person who writes to you wishes for a moment when he can cry over everything that the war has taken away and recover from the darkness that is eating him.

The frightened person who writes now wishes to be a very ordinary person, nothing more.

My Daughter Nai

My three-year-old daughter Nai, whose twin, Majd, lives in Turkey for treatment due to an enlarged liver. And his constant need for medical care teaches me that life can be dealt with as long as one is alive. She does not know that we have been living under the threat of death for the past 400 days; that we are forced to live without her brother Majd, and without her grandmother Aida, who accompanies Majd, and receives treatment for breast cancer, without her uncle Mohammed and his family who travelled to Egypt to escape the war.

Nai knows very well that she wants to interact with life without giving attention to the loved ones, relatives and friends we lose every hour. Without giving attention that we are forced to live in an area located on the beach. Nai receives life as if it is without deficiency, and I seek her help to save me and heal me from the deficiency and the loss of everything I once owned.

I have a story to tell about words, words that have disappeared. All the places, streets, landmarks and maps of the place are a language that I have been forced not to use for 401 days. I say the name of the place 'Gaza City' but I cannot sit in a taxi and tell the driver to drop me off at the university traffic signal, the Saraya traffic signal, the Legislative Council intersection, the Families Roundabout, Omar Al-Mukhtar Street, or Al-Wahda Street—without listing every address I once used to navigate the Gaza Strip. I also lost the means of using a language that contains words that I used to describe my life.

I stopped using words and phrases like 'We are pleased to invite you to attend an event at Gallery 28 or Beit Al-Ghussein', 'a vacation in a chalet', 'I requested a car', 'delivery', 'supermarket', 'shop', 'restaurant', and so on, until all the names of restaurants, companies and shops finished.

I have a story to tell about the genocide: how it destroyed all the worlds that we once knew inside the Gaza Strip; how by managing our lives we built temporary worlds while the genocide continued; and how we will always choose life and hope for the end of the war and the return of life.

I wonder what worlds we will rebuild? What new worlds will we build?

Mahmoud Alshaer is an editor, curator, and poet from Rafah, who, until October 2023, was deeply involved in cultural work in Gaza, leading initiatives such as Majalla 28 and Gallery 28 and coordinating the cultural program at Al Ghussein Cultural House in Gaza's old city. He is one of the curators of this book, as he recognized that a vital need of the hour was to consolidate the reality and experiences of this war for posterity. On October 2024, his twin children Majd and Nia celebrated their third birthday, separately in different countries, after one whole year of growing up in war. Mahmoud, his wife Hadil, and their daughter Nia were injured by six Israeli airstrikes on their home and have since been in a humanitarian zone.

Despite such excruciating challenges, Mahmoud has diligently worked to bring this collection to life and prioritized every possible challenge. It has given him a sense of purpose and helped him see light in dark hours; as he himself says, *I ask you to share our story, to spread the word about the ongoing devastation in Gaza. Let the world know that we are still here, still fighting, still in need of your voices and your support.*

AFTERWORD

Year of Pain
by Elias Khoury
Translated by Leonie Böttiger

It surprised me to realize I've been languishing in a hospital bed for an entire year.

It's a life of pain that stops only for new pain, as if a person were made of intersecting materials, and the pains of each of them reshape their lives. I shouldn't complain, and I'm not complaining. But the intensity of this pain could shatter stones, and it empties life of all meaning. In our regular everyday lives, we need to search for meaning. But in the life of pain, we must create meaning. Who creates meaning if not those who have been scalded by unending pain?

When I wake up to write my weekly column, a doubled pain explodes inside me, as if I had committed all the sins and crimes since the dawn of time. I can't describe the pain—it's a feeling that hits you like a surprise, and then, when it lets up for a moment, leaves you in lifeless pieces. No one has described the pain or written about it: we are immersed in the unwritable.

In a world of sorrow, we hope for a quick end, so that we can hurry back to a life that has lost all taste and pleasure, but which we haven't forgotten and won't forget. I imagine before me a sea of pain, raging against me, striking me from all sides while I scream. I am now waiting for time—a slow, heavy, and repulsive time that does not come. But in the end, it will arrive by force. We will bring it in chains to testify that our right to live is sacred. I won't take you back to the pains of Lord Jesus or those of Mary Magdalene, but I will tell you that it's an immense trial, and I am right in the middle of it.

Do you know anyone who has written pain? Show me who they are, so they can keep me company on this journey of agony that I have embarked upon alone. Send them to me, so I can read them my story and listen to theirs. Except, when I find someone like this, I see that they flinch from me, that they are afraid to confront my pain and their own, as if the pains don't intersect.

Is the head separate from the body?

Can I think with my head while my body is torn to pieces?

This is pain's game with me. I begin to write, and I feel a calmness of the spirit descend upon me, from head to body, but moments later, this serenity is tangled with the brutal pain that overwhelms me and forces me to stop and recover my clarity. This game has exhausted me, and I don't know how to play it. All I can do is to turn toward it for help, to look for some safe place within. Is there a safe space when pain lashes you? I don't know. None of us know, but we try to maintain some minimal relationship between the head and the body.

I remember July 12, 2023, when I stood in the emergency room of the Hôtel-Dieu Hospital, and was suddenly struck by a pain no human could bear. I begged the nurse for morphine, and then I begged for death so that this pain would stop. Then I lost consciousness and found myself, two days later, in intensive care. The pain had no precedent, and I hadn't imagined it could exist with such ferocity, but there it was, ambushing me.

It had been the night of my birthday, and my daughter had prepared a celebration, but the feast suddenly turned into its opposite, a wedding of pain. Do you remember? I no longer have the energy to remember. Right now, I'm in bed telling you what I felt that day and the days that followed. I don't want you to forget that pain can come out of nowhere and settle in our bodies and souls and make itself at home among us. Despite all this, I didn't lose courage or hope.

How can someone lose hope when they are surrounded by friends and loved ones, and when they experience an unparalleled love? How could I, when I had a whole group of doctors who devoted their time to saving me? How could someone lose courage, when their experience has been mixed in, since the beginning, with the clay of Palestinian resistance?

Gaza and Palestine have been brutally bombarded for almost a year now, too, and they are steadfast. Unshakeable. They are the model from which I learn, every day, to love life.

*

Lebanese novelist **Elias Khoury** has dedicated much of his work to the Palestinian cause and has taught at universities worldwide, establishing himself as one of Lebanon's leading intellectuals. In 2000, he received the Prize of Palestine for his novel *Gate of the Sun*, and in 2007, he was awarded the Al Owais Prize for fiction. He passed away in September 2024, a year after the start of the war in Gaza.

Born almost exactly two months after what is known as the Nakba, Elias Khoury's life as an intellectual, a novelist, and a human being, was deeply shaped by it. His embrace of the Palestinian cause often confuses readers who assume, based on the passion and vividness of his novels about Palestine, that Elias is Palestinian. While he may not have been Palestinian by birth, Elias Khoury is undoubtedly as Palestinian at heart, as he is Lebanese.

The novel that brought him international recognition is, arguably, *Gate of the Sun*, a moving, sweeping epic that, through its many characters, depicts the continuous nature of the Nakba, capturing its human dimension, and giving ordinary Palestinians the voice they were deprived from. *Gate of the Sun* tells the story of Khalil, who cares for Younes. Khalil's love for Younes is that of a son for his father. Younes's life is characterized by resistance and defiance, as well as a beautiful love story with his wife, who remained in Palestine. Younes would secretly meet with her in Palestine, in a cave called Bab al Shams, or *Gate of the Sun*.

The relationship between narration and life is a recurrent theme in Elias Khoury's writing. Little did he know, when he wrote *Gate of the Sun*, that his beautiful story would inspire Palestinians and bring this imaginary place to life.

In 2013, around 250 young men and women from various parts of Palestine gathered in a region east of Jerusalem, referred to as 'E1' by the Israeli authorities. They decided to create a town as an act of resistance, and this town was too named 'Bab al Shams', or 'Gate of the Sun'.

Not only does the world shape our life stories, but some of our stories also shape the world. Both these facts are true of Elias Khoury's unique relationship with Palestine and the Palestinians.

ACKNOWLEDGEMENTS

This book would not have been possible without the courage and resilience of the writers and artists who, despite the horrors of war and displacement, shared their words. We are deeply grateful to every contributor who entrusted us with his or her stories, testimonies, and visions of life under genocide.

Our sincere appreciation to Marcia Lynx Qualey for her unwavering commitment to Palestinian voices, to our commissioning editor Sarah Zia for her unrelenting belief in this project, and to the team at Penguin Random House for all their support and ensuring it reaches readers across the globe.

It's not just a book—it's our voice, made possible through this incredible partnership.

A special thank you to our translator Wiam El-Tamami, and everyone who worked tirelessly to bring this book to life.

Lastly, to our readers—this book is an act of remembrance and resistance. Thank you for holding these stories, for bearing witness, and for ensuring that the truth endures.

—**Mahmoud Alshaer and Mohammed Al-Zaqzooq**

***

Publishers are chroniclers of history; we bear witness to the defining events of our times and archive them for posterity. The journey of collecting real-time war writings is a daunting one with many challenges. Achieving this feat would not have been possible without the inexhaustible efforts and dedication of all the individuals who came together to bring this book to life.

The most heartfelt thanks to our writers in Gaza, who have persevered to ensure their writings reach us despite the dire circumstances. They have written through their grief, their silences and their cries; and we are immensely grateful to them for entrusting us with their personal writings.

A sincere thanks to the team at *ArabLit Quarterly* by Marcia Lynx Qualey, who aided communication with the writers in Gaza and helped with the translation of all the writings. All our writers in Gaza were dispersed across the Strip due to displacements, which meant at times we could only pray for their well-being without any contact for weeks. It was immensely reassuring to have *ArabLit* work with us to ensure the project moved along despite the challenges.

To our team of translators, thank you for beautifully and authentically bringing these letters to life. Thank you to Nour Ziada, our brilliant illustrator from Gaza, for the evocative cover art.

A massive thanks to the stalwart Atef Abu Saif for the moving introduction, which comprehensively defines the importance of this book, and of the people of Gaza being able to tell their stories in their words. We highly value your time and contribution to this project.

We are grateful to the generous Yasmina Jraissati, literary agent and niece of late Elias Khoury, the legendary writer from Lebanon, for sharing his last unpublished article. Elias holds a special place for the people of Palestine and especially for our writers; we are honoured to publish his last writing posthumously.

Lastly, but not the least, a huge shout-out to all the teams at Penguin Random House, who came together and worked incredibly hard to bring this book to our readers.

And to our readers, we constantly strive to bring you books with deep meaning and significance; we hope *Letters from Gaza* continues to be a book that makes you proud to be a Penguin reader.

—Penguin Random House

LETTERS TO GAZA

Sharing a warm smile, a kind word, and thoughts laced with prayers and togetherness can be the most powerful acts of kindness. The people of Gaza have opened their hearts to us, let's now envelop them with our love and compassion.

Please share your thoughts and messages with them, below and via email. As they navigate this journey, let our words be a source of strength, and build a community of compassion around them.

Email : lettersfromgaza.mm@gmail.com